THE BOOK OF
HIGH BICKINGTON

A DEVON RIDGEWAY PARISH
AVRIL STONE

HALSGROVE

First published in Great Britain in 2000

THE BOOK OF HIGH BICKINGTON IS DEDICATED TO THE
MEMORY OF MY MOTHER, ETHEL BARTHRAM, WHOSE LOVE
AND SUPPORT ENCOURAGED ME TO TAKE ON THE
IMPOSSIBLE AND ACHIEVE THE UNBELIEVABLE.
SHE DIED THE DAY AFTER I FINISHED THIS BOOK.

British Library Cataloguing-in-Publication Data
A CIP record for this title is available from the British Library

ISBN 1 84114 061 9

HALSGROVE
PUBLISHING, MEDIA AND DISTRIBUTION

Halsgrove House
Lower Moor Way
Tiverton, Devon EX16 6SS
Tel: 01884 243242
Fax: 01884 243325
email: sales@halsgrove.com
website: http://www.halsgrove.com

Printed and bound in Great Britain by Bookcraft Ltd., Midsomer Norton

Foreword

There are few greater compliments a writer can pay than to focus their artistic energies on the community in which they live. A study such as this volume pays testament to an enduring interest in, and love of, the locality. To my mind it is also indicative of some not inconsiderable element of bravery; there is certainly no escape for the local author - especially when it comes to the inevitable quibbles over dates, names and other such details that fall prey to the inaccuracies of human memory.

Time will inevitably blur facts and distort once clear stories, but in Avril's case one can be sure that every aspect of the High Bickington story has been drawn together as carefully as possible. This she has done with some trepidation - the present title is her first publication - but also with the help of numerous members of the community, near and far. Memories and photographs have been lent by countless families and individuals across the parish who have given freely of their time and memorabilia, keen to help with the project.

The end result stands as a celebration of High Bickington and one that is truly of, and for, the parish community - past, present and future.

NAOMI CUDMORE
MANAGING EDITOR, COMMUNITY HISTORIES
HALSGROVE, 2000

Dr Good starting the girls under 10 years race at the Sports Day, 1923.

PREFACE

The seed of the idea for this book was sown when I was on a day-a-week course in art and design at the North Devon College. But little did I realise it then!

While at the college I was introduced to the work of James Ravilious - a photographer with an almost magical ability to capture people going about their everyday pursuits unaware of his camera. He was later to tell me how he achieved this, and was generous with his advice and encouragement.

Since childhood I have been a keen photographer and part of the college course was an exercise to interpret 'Devon Life' in photographs. Where better than my own village? As I walked around High Bickington with my camera I discovered that what I had imagined was a dormitory for our local towns was in fact a vibrant community. The suggestion was made that I should combine a study in pictures with an account of life in our parish over the past century - a daunting challenge! However, it turned out to be the most inspiring and interesting time of my life.

This book is not an academic history of High Bickington. It is the stories of the people who make up our parish today and of those who made up its yesterdays. I hope you enjoy reading them as much as I have enjoyed collecting them.

AVRIL STONE
HIGH BICKINGTON, 2000

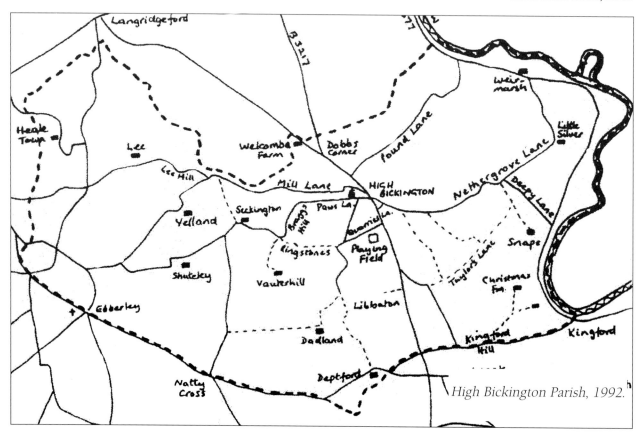

High Bickington Parish, 1992.

CONTENTS

Taking a break for lunch during a shoot at Nethergrove. Dr Gussy Greenwood-Penny, Dr Arnold Saxty Good and the gamekeeper, 1904.

Bill Pidler on his Shire horse at Witherhill, c.1920.

Acknowledgements

The first meeting about our book was held in the Church Hall on a wet November night. There was an interesting football match on the TV yet surprisingly more than 40 people came to hear the ideas for this project. From that day on there was a rich and constant stream of photographs, memorabilia and anecdotes. It led, too, to the formation of High Bickington Historical Society (whose first year aim was to help with research and fund-raising for this book). Long may they flourish!

And so to the people whose assistance I want to acknowledge specially. My warm thanks to: Sydney Squire for the information he has shared with me about his long and varied life in the village. It was his pleasure in recounting memories of his younger days that inspired this book; Margaret Bolt who lent me all her scrapbooks of events in the parish, did much research and was always on the end of the phone ready to answer my queries and give her support; Richard Lethbridge for the loan of his researches from local newspapers with their interesting and often amusing stories which I have been able to use, and for his photographs taken around the parish; the Parochial Church Council for access to their minutes book going back more than a century. Also High Bickington Athletic Club for sight of their records.

I thank Philip Keen for his excellent sketches to illustrate some of the stories; Keith Herbert for creating a superb web-site and for all his patience with this computer illiterate; Tim Pugsley and Andy Robinson for their photographic advice and encouragement; Stan Tucker for the loan of his grandfather's diary; Edgar Cole for the contents of PC Garland's essay; and Mary Good for her family narrative and photographs.

Also: Roy Hopkins, the wartime evacuee, who tells a moving story of a little boy's insight into village life. I wish there was space to use everything he wrote; the friend who read all my work and spent hours giving the grammar 'a quick going over' (as she puts it). Praise and encouragement were there whenever I needed it.

Permission to use photographs taken by R.L. Knight (credited R.L.K.) was granted by Knight's Photographers; S.H. Bath (S.H.B.) by Bath Photographic. Beaford Archive photographs were used with their kind permission. Photographs taken by Richard Lethbridge are marked (R.L.), Graham Walker (G.W.) and Avril Stone (A.S.). I also referred to the following titles: *St Mary's Church Guide Book*, *High Bickington Methodist Church, 1834-1984: A Brief History*, *Tom Wills' Bus* and the *North Devon Journal*.

For the loan of photographs, documents and additional research I have to thank: Alan and Don Assheton, Charlie Ball, Barbara Barrett, Brian Barrow, John Barthram, Jim Bright, Liam Bunclarke, Stella and Ken Burrows, Helen Carn, Revd John Carvosso, Edgar Cole, Sam Couch, Mrs E.M. Curtis, John Down, Kathleen Down, Christine England, Edward Eyres, Peggy Field, Margaret and Richard Gayton, Pauline and George German, Jane Gibson, Dorothy Gill, Revd Vincent Gillett, Jennifer Gooding, Dave Gumm, Derek Herniman, Wendy Herniman, Shirley and John Hill, Mary Hymas, Hazel Keen, Roger Keen, Ann Lawson, Tom and May Miller, John Mulvey, Rosemary Munson, Betty Netherway, Toby and Jacquline Newth, James Parker, Stan and Una Parker, Bert Parsons, Dick and Sylvia Pidler, Ken and Penny Povey, Maurice and Doreen Ridd, Myc and Jenny Riggulsford, Jackie Rudman, Bunny and Gerald Snell, Keith and Diana Snell, Margaret Squire, Hannah St John, Vera Stevens, Jean Tapscott, Liz Taynton, Mark and Nina Thomas, Glenda Tucker, Stan and Eileen Tucker, Joyce Underhill, Grahan Walker, Jim and Lorna Ward, Tim Webb, Iris Wickett and Vida Wonnacott.

Last, but by no means least, my love and thanks go to my supportive family, especially to my husband Eric for putting up with my 'artistic' temperament, for being a telephone answering service and for not complaining at the burnt offerings I've served him over the past year!

AVRIL STONE

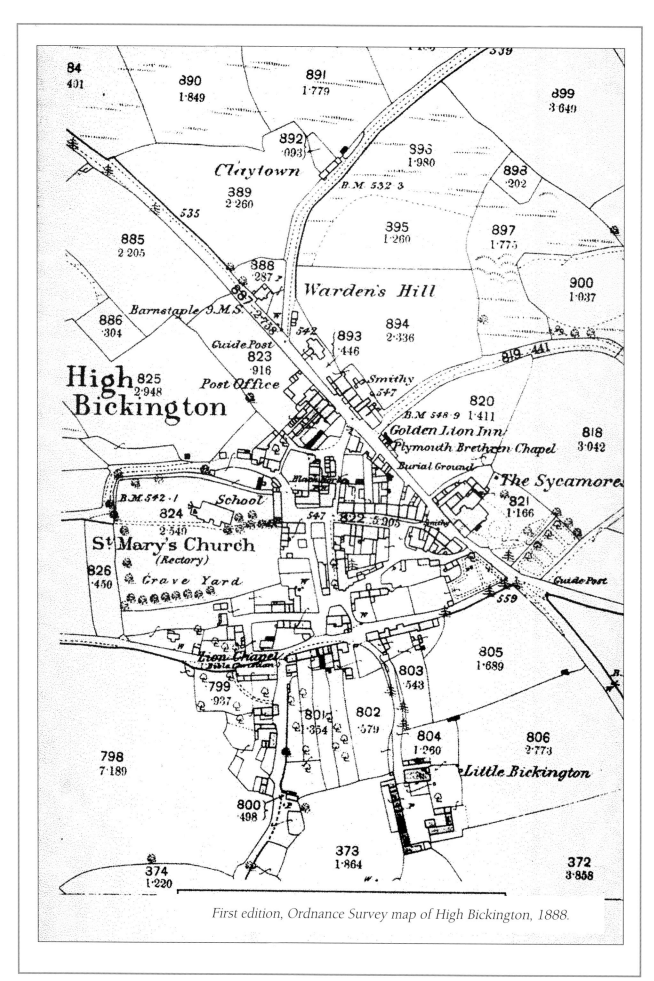

First edition, Ordnance Survey map of High Bickington, 1888.

Chapter 1
Early History

The story of High Bickington probably starts more than 1000 years ago. Before that it is thought this whole area was a forest. The ancient Britons may have had a settlement here, but as no proof of such remains we can only assume that the Saxons were the first inhabitants of the parish.

In this chapter I am grateful for the booklets written by R.W. Pitman in 1937, when he was schoolmaster at High Bickington School, and Major E.J. Winter in his *Brief History of St Mary's Church, High Bickington*.

THE SAXONS

Although the Saxons began arriving in Britain about AD400 it was late in AD650 before they conquered and settled in the Vale of Taunton. Around AD690 they arrived in Exeter. North Devon was settled by an advance from Somerset, so the earliest settlement at High Bickington must have been c.AD700.

There may be some difference of opinion as to the exact meaning of the name High Bickington, but the most popular idea is that Bickington (Bichentone in the Domesday Book) means settlement or farm of the sons (or tribe) of Beocca. We can conclude that Beocca was our first Saxon landlord.

'High' does not need any explanation, especially for those of us who live here on cold, wet winter days when the wind is blowing from the east! For further proof of Saxon settlers we may look at the explanation of the place names, which fall into three groups:

* Those named after the owner, as in Beocca, the owner of Bichentone; Dadland, after Doda a farmer who arrived with Beocca or who succeeded him; Seckington, which means 'the land of a litigious person'; and Snape, after Galfride de Snape (whose daughter married Baghill, owner of Stowford).

* Those names which are natural descriptions - Gratley, a great cleave or steep slope; Deptford, a deep ford; and Stowford, a staved, banked or stoney ford; Shuteley, a jutting out place or promontory (although another scholastic book on Saxon place names has Shuteley as a clearing in a wood belonging to a man named Shute).

* Those with farming names - Lee, meadowland; Week, a farm or dwelling on the outskirts of the parish; and Yelland, from 'ye old land', which is either land long cultivated, gone out of cultivation or worn out.

High Bickington may have been a typical Saxon settlement with all of the dwellings grouped together in the centre and the arable land surrounding it. Another idea is that it may have been several hamlets and large farms clustered around the same area - High Bickington, Seckington, Hele, Stowford and Holt. Such a theory may be supported by the fact that in Norman times we read of the manors of Stowford, Snape, Clavil Holt and Loges. These hamlets or manors would have been consolidated in AD930 when King Athelstane founded the Church at High Bickington. King Athelstane also gave the gift of a 'holt', the Saxon word for a great wood or forest, which in turn supports the theory that this area was forested.

In the early-17th century Tristram Risdon the antiquary, who was born at St Giles in the Wood and complied *A Survey of Devon*, noted that the woods which used to exist on both sides of the River Taw, and in which herds of swine had lived, had by this time been cut down - which led to this poetical lament:

Under lofty tower'd trees, in times that are
    forepast,
Did the savage swine let fall their larding mast,
But now, alas! Ourselves we have not to sustain,
And safeguard we have none to keep us from
    the rain,

Such changes of the world that since our youth befel,
This naked nook of land, 'twere grievous for to tell;
Where, fearless of the hunt, the deer securely stood,
And tripping freely, walked a burgess of the wood.

We still have an area in the parish called 'Great Wood', on the hillside overlooking the river valley (and no doubt the subject of Risdon's lament). Unfortunately it is probably no more wooded in the 21st century than it was in the 1700s.

BRICTRIC

Before the Norman Conquest in 1066 High Bickington was in the possession of a Saxon called Brictric. He also owned land revenues of Gloucester and extensive estates in the West Country.

Brictric was sent on a diplomatic mission to Flanders and whilst there Matilda the Duke of Flanders' daughter fell madly and passionately in love with him. She offered herself in matrimony to the handsome Saxon but Brictric rejected her offer and returned to England - a decision which was to prove unfortunate for him.

Matilda later married a rather unpleasant chap called William the Bastard, The Duke of Normandy, and the story goes that Matilda only agreed to marry him after he beat her into submission. It could be said that poor Matilda was not having much luck in the love stakes. William, being a direct descendant of the Viking sea adventurers, was a skilled and ruthless warrior. He invaded England, was crowned King and therefore Matilda was Queen.

With all the revenge of a woman scorned, Matilda demanded Brictric's arrest. He was imprisoned in Winchester and met a very slow and painful death. Naturally, all his lands and estates passed to Matilda. These, named in the Domesday Book, included: Bichentone, Clovelly, Bideford, Winkleigh, Tiverton, Lew, Halwill, Littleham, Langtree, Iddesleigh, Ash, Lapford, Alwardsdone, Morchard, Holcombe, Halberton and Washburton. They all became part of the Honour of Gloucester. A lesson could be learnt here, that a gentleman should think twice before rejecting a lady with romantic intentions!

There are two accounts of Bichentone in the Domesday Book, one in the Exchequer copy and one in the Exeter copy. The latter includes the following:

The King has a manor called Bichentone which Brictric held on the day on which King Edward was alive and dead, and it paid geld for one hide and a half, and half a virgate; these can be ploughed by 16 ploughs; of these the King has one virgate and two ploughs in demesne, and the villeins have five virgates and half and seven ploughs. There the King has 14 villeins, two borders, three serfs and two swineherds who render 16 swine yearly; 12 head of cattle and 50 sheep. And 100 acres of meadow and 100 acres of pasture. And it renders yearly £12.

Mention is also made of the fact that to this manor was added a manor called Bicheneleia (Langley) which in the time of King Edward belonged to Tauestoca (Tawstock) and that it rendered £4 to Bichentone.

As much of the terminology is now unfamiliar to us it is hoped that the following will serve as an approximate interpretation: geld = paid tax on; hide = approximately 120 acres; virgate = a quarter of a hide; demesne = land held by the lord of the manor for his own benefit (he did not have to pay any tax to the king); villeins = peasant farmers/villagers; borders = less than peasants (extremely poor); serfs or slaves = owned by the lord of the manor. For the measurement of a plough I have come across different explanations but it is probably safe to say that land for one plough meant in Devon about 64 acres, or 80 acres including roads, hedges and waste land.

From this entry in the Domesday Book we can assume that High Bickington had approximately 1000 acres, considerably less than today.

CHANGING LANDLORDS

In 1083 Matilda's son William Rufus, later William II, inherited the lands his mother had taken after Brictric's fateful demise and gave Bichentone to Robert Fitzhamon. William was succeeded by his younger brother Henry I who married off Fitzhamon's eldest daughter Maud to his illegitimate son Robert. To enable him to inherit the whole estate Maud's three sisters and co-heiresses were put in a convent in Shaftesbury.

By 1150 the manor of High Bickington was in the possession of the Champernownes of Umberleigh. Lady Joan Champernowne (who must have been the forerunner of the Women's Lib Movement!) insisted that her sons kept her maiden name and coat of arms rather than that of their father, Sir Ralph Willingdon. It is interesting to note that two of Sir Ralph's relatives were later rectors in High Bickington, Robert de Wyllyntone in 1308 and Sir Robert de Wyllyntone in 1315. Lady Champernowne had the Chantry built at Atherington and for a reason undisclosed she gave some of her lands, including Holt, to the Loges family.

During the reign of King John (1199-1261) Hugh de Loges owned the manor of Buckington Loges. Eventually this passed down through the family from

Hugh to Roger, William and Walter and finally in 1316 to a William Boyes. At this time we find references of several manors, such as Holt, Loges, Snape, Stowford and Clavil, which were owned by William de Fulford and Robert de Leghe. There was also Corpsland, which was the Church Manor, and adjoining the parish, Buryet and Wootton. Many of these place names are still in existence today.

Times were changing and from about the middle of the 12th century rents were paid in cash and not in kind, as the reference in the Domesday Book shows us when it states that the swineherd paid 16 swine yearly. Eventually, as the land-owners found need for more funds, they sold off parcels of land and the estates began to be divided.

In 1498 Buckington Clavil was held by a group of five, including William Paul, John Gyre, William Godman, Galfrid at Knowle and John Juyll, and the property, as it was then written 'they [held] separately amongst themselves and none of them [held] more than a quarter part and which of old Rodulph of Appledore held'.

Although many manors were being sold off the parson held ownership of Corpsland (the Church Manor) up until the early 1800s. This included the property known as 'Parsonage' which was a farm and is now a private dwelling. However, the rector did not necessarily live here as we find that in 1700 he was at a large farm near the present Beechwood House, which was later built as the Rectory.

It is not recorded how the ownership of the farms changed but they were obviously split up and sold. However, there were still a few large land-owners, such as the Bassetts of Umberleigh who inherited lands from the Champernownes (lands which were disposed of between 1800 and 1900).

From the 15th century onwards the Pyncombes of North Molton amassed much of the land surrounding High Bickington. The last surviving member of this family was Gertrude Pyncombe who in her will of 20 January 1730 founded a charitable educational trust from which grants are still made to this day. After the First World War the Church estates were sold and the trustees of the Pyncombe Estate sold all their properties at an auction which was held at the village school on 26 November 1919.

THE AGRICULTURAL REVOLUTION

Back in the 1700s the poorer man who had previously kept a cow or a pig on common land lost his right to do so. Machinery was also beginning to be used on farms and there was less work available for farm labourers. As they lost their jobs or became too old or ill to work they grew to be a burden on the the parish which had to keep them on the Poor Rate. This was a double-edged sword as it meant that people could not leave their own parish to look for work because no other parish would take responsibility for them.

When travelling to another area the poor had to go before a justice of the peace and swear on oath as to their place of birth to enable them to get Relief. There is a case documented in the church register dated 1698 concerning a request from High Bickington to Atherington that a labourer and his family be permitted to go and live in Atherington where he had found work and guaranteeing to receive him back and look after him and his family should he become a charge on the Poor Rate.

In July 1865 a local newspaper reported that a mother was summoned at the insistence of the Board of Guardians of the Torrington Union and accused of deserting her child and leaving it chargeable to the parish of High Bickington. The Bench ordered the defendant to be apprehended and committed to a house of correction for one month.

Every year the parish overseers, usually two in number, were appointed. Again in the same newspaper we read that:

... at the Divisional Petty Session, William Purchase who was second on the list, objected on the ground that he could not read or write. The Bench informed him that if he could not do it himself he would have to find someone to take his place. However as he had only been in the parish for three years they appointed William Brownscombe whose name was next on the list. Mr Purchase was informed that if his name were on the list next year he would have to do his duty.

This was obviously not a sought-after post!

In the 1800s High Bickington was still a mainly self-sufficient community, although as stated in *Billings Directory and Gazetteer of the County of Devon 1857*, the market at Torrington was 'excellent for meat, poultry, butter, eggs, etc., which quality cannot be surpassed by any town in Devon'. High Bickington folk would travel to Torrington to buy goods that were not available at home and to sell their surplus produce.

Due to the decline in the labour market from 1850 many people from the countryside emigrated to America, Canada and Australia. The population of High Bickington in 1801 was 693 rising to 851 by 1851. In 1891 there were 583 people living in the parish (288 males and 295 females) and housed in 124 dwellings. There were 25 uninhabited houses which gives a good indication of the declining numbers from the mid-19th century onwards. By 1901 the population had fallen to 539 and in the 1950s reached its lowest point of 410. The last electoral roll registered 521.

Millbrook in 2000, which was originally Pulley Mills, the corn mill owned by the Pyncombe Charity Trust. (A.S.)

Main picture: *Weir Marsh Farm with Eli Harris and his family, c.1900.*
Inset: *Peter May and his mother Margaret at Weir Marsh, 2000.* (A.S.)

Chapter 2
A Tour of the Parish

High Bickington lies ten miles south east of Barnstaple, the largest town in North Devon. The small market town of South Molton is ten miles to the north. Eight miles in the opposite direction is the historic town of Torrington. At 600 feet above sea level the prefix 'High' is well deserved. To the north we can view the passing shades of Exmoor and to the south, although further away, stands Dartmoor clearly visible and imposingly grand.

GEOLOGY

High Bickington lies on Carboniferous rocks, sometimes called Culm Measures. The topmost rocks are Welcombe Formation, which is shale and thin sandstone. Under this is Bude Formation and then Crackington Formation which is principally shale and thin sandstone. The presence of shale gives rise to poorly drained clayey soils, typically on flat hilltops, where rough, rush-covered pastures are found. This landscape is most evident on the southern side of the parish where the ground is extremely difficult to cultivate. The marsh ground along the Taw River consists of brown, deep loam on loose black gravel and sand.

The highest point of the parish is Ebberley at 640 feet and the next highest is Windy Castle. The average annual rainfall is 43.06 inches.

BEATING THE BOUNDS

In this chapter we will circumnavigate the parish as in the ancient tradition of beating the bounds. As far back as the 5th century people would walk the parish limits as a fertility rite; and later it became a civic tradition to confirm the boundary. The younger folk had to be shown the parish fringes and, along the way, endure hardships such as being pulled through hedges, pushed up trees and dunked in

Eli Harris and wife Elizabeth (née Cole) with their eight children, c.1880. They lived at Weirmarsh Farm.

streams and ponds to impress on them the danger of straying 'out of bounds' or going 'beyond their limits' - expressions we are all familiar with.

Like any other parish High Bickington's boundary follows either roads which used to be pack-horse paths, sheep trails or natural features such as rivers or streams. It is several years since we had a beating of the bounds in High Bickington. However, I am helped in this chapter by David Venner, a local environmentalist who did it on his own in 1990.

We start at the north-west point of the parish, near Smallmarsh on the A377 just outside Umberleigh. The boundary runs alongside the river with the road and railway line in close formation until we arrive at Kingford Bridge. Along this first stretch of the road the hillside on the right once boasted many market gardens as it was excellent ground with sheltered conditions for fruit growing. Evidence of this can be found in the account book of William and Jane Eastman who lived at Smallmarsh Farm. Here we see names of fruits long forgotten and removed from the supermarket shelves, apples with names such as Annie Elizabeth, Prince Albert, Rilston Pippins, Morgans Sweet and Blenheim Orange, and soft fruits such as strawberries, gooseberries, cherries and mazzards. Mrs Clatworthy, who lives at Little Smallmarsh, remembers her husband Ern sitting under the mazzard trees to scare off the birds. Bullfinches, or 'hoops' as they were called, were the worst. I am reliably informed that a mazzard tastes better than any black cherry. When cooked in a pie they set in their own jelly. It seems a great pity that this delicacy is in rare supply today.

Further along the road we pass Pound Lane and Shoplands Lane, leaving the village perched high on the ridge above. On our left we have Weirmarsh Farm, named after two previous owners and built

Above: *Higher Deptford Farm, 1940s.*

Above: *Rose Cottage, c.1920. Kitty Way with her father George Way who was the signalman at Portsmouth Arms Station.*

Above: *Cars stopped at Rose Cottage, to buy wild spring daffodils. Left to right, standing: Kit Davis, her sister Beattie Way, Herbert Eastman.*

Above: *Marwood House Hotel under renovation, 1890. Left to right: Lily Way, Mabel Way, Beatrice Way, Reg Trigger; James Leythorne (on building).*

Right: *Postcard of Kingford sent to Miss Beattie Way from her brother Albert. The people in the picture may be the Way family outside their home, Rose Cottage, after 1908. The signpost points to the left so the bridge must have been built by then.*

Pulley Mills (now Milbrook) with Jack Kent on the left and William Pidler on the right., c.1920.

here after the construction of the railway during the course of which the original building (centuries earlier a manor called Holt) was destroyed. Eli Harris lived with his wife and eight children at Weirmarsh for most of his 86 years and died in 1926. He was a stalwart of High Bickington society, a churchwarden for 37 years and a renowned horticulturalist. He was also a keen sportsman in the hunting and shooting field. Today the farm is run by Peter May and his family. Everyone who travels this road knows the sign outside the farm for 'Farmer May's Spuds'.

The steep-sided valley now becomes wooded. Names such as Weir Marsh Wood, Greathill Wood, Snape Wood and Great Wood and farms and houses called Middlewood, Northwood, Southwood, and Beechwood recall ancient times when the area was forested. Perhaps this is also where our district ward name of Great Wood originated.

KINGFORD   Kingford is an attractive hamlet. Unfortunately when you pass through it by car you are usually travelling too fast to appreciate it! Marwood House on the right used to be a public house, and it was here that Mrs Barton from Kingford Hill had a water pipe and outside tap installed for the use of everyone who lived in the vicinity.

Rose Cottage on the left was where George Way, the railway signalman for Portsmouth Arms, lived with his wife and nine children. These two houses are fondly remembered for the bowls of flowers, especially daffodils in springtime, on sale outside.

We come now to a crossroads and the furthest point east of our boundary. The road to the left would take us over Kingford Bridge and the River Taw to Chittlehamholt on the summit of the other side of the valley. However, we turn right here and travel up the wooded hillside, passing through

Colebrook Wood and Upcott Wood, until we arrive at the crossroads at the top of the hill at Week Park Cross. We carry on across the main road past Great Deptford House which was once farmed by Tom and May Miller and is now an extremely desirable residence. Over Deptford Bridge the boundary leaves the road for a short while and follows the stream. It rejoins it again before we arrive at Natty Cross – the name of which remains, at the time of writing, a mystery.

EBBERLEY At 640 feet above sea level there are breathtaking views for miles around, and after walking up from the bottom of the valley you may feel that you wish you had brought a spare oxygen tank! The air is definitely crisper and usually blowing several knots faster in this exposed part of the parish. To walk this road early on a hot summer morning, with a cloudless sky, larks singing and not a soul in sight or sound, you feel you must have found heaven.

There are very few trees in this area and the poorly drained rough grassland tends to be boggy due to the carboniferous rock and impervious clay soil. The road is again the boundary line. On one side we have High Bickington and on the other the parish of Roborough. To confuse the issue even more, St Giles in the Wood is the postal address for all of the houses along this road. Three lanes from the village join this road, one of which has travelled through the hamlet of Seckington and another of these branches off at Seckington to pass Shuteley and join the third which comes from Yelland Farm. This last lane leaves the village behind St Mary's Church as Mill Lane.   The roads radiate from the centre of the village and as you look at the map of the parish it appears as a giant cartwheel with the spokes leaving the central hub.

At Ebberley Hill crossroads stands a large Georgian house which was once the Ebberley Arms Hotel where Mr James Knight, described at the trial for his murder as an itinerant quack doctor, was killed on the cold and frosty night of 30 March 1837. After the trial of only circumstantial evidence the jury took just 20 minutes to find Robert Alford of Vaulterhill Farm guilty of manslaughter. He was sentenced to be 'transported to parts beyond the seas for the term of his natural life'.

From the crossroads the road continues straight on past the houses at High Down and the site of another public house, the 'New Inn', long since disappeared. Shortly after the next crossroads the boundary turns northwards over the fields towards the corner of the parish called North Heale.

NORTH HEALE   This part of the parish boundary lies deep in wooded valleys and follows the streams that make up Langley Brook. I have not walked this area, but David Venner has. He wrote that in May when he walked this route the wider reaches of these valleys contained damp rushy meadows, their lush verdant green splashed with the lilac of Lady's Smock and the bright yellow of Marsh Marigolds.

In this corner of the parish are a number of farms, including South Heale, Heale Town, North Heale and Commons Farm. At this point we join with our neighbouring parishes of Atherington and Yarnscombe, where two streams meet. At the base of the one-in-four hill at Langridgeford we turn eastwards to return to our village.

The last lap of our journey takes us once again along the river path through the wooded valley below the farms of Lee and Lee Barton, with the road from Langridgeford to High Bickington on the other side. At the ford at the bottom of Millbrook, which was once a corn mill called Pulley Mills, the boundary does a sharp turn like a dog's hind leg to follow the stream that comes out at Welcombe Farm. Across a field, over the main road which enters the village from Atherington, and then following another stream, we travel through another Great Wood (although whether this is of any relation to the one on the other side of the village remains unknown). Finally, we come back to Smallmarsh where we started our perambulation care of David Venner.

Top: *View of Dobbs with Welcombe Farm on the left.* (R.L.K.)

Right: *David Venner making a garden pyramid using Devon hazelwood, 1999.* (A.S.)

Chapter 3
A Walk Around the Village

High Bickington village sits on top of a ridge overlooking the River Taw Valley and commands beautiful and dramatic views whatever the season. Old houses nestle cosily around the ancient church of St Mary's like a group of old ladies gathered around a fire for warmth and comfort.

The main road, North Road, skirts the northern fringe of the village and you could be excused for travelling through without realising how interesting and attractive the inner village really is.

NORTH ROAD

We will start our perambulation from the direction of Barnstaple. Standing here at the gateway of the village we have a crossroads. The road on the right would take us into Barton Meadow, which until a year ago was a cul-de-sac with some two dozen houses on a small modern estate. However, the road has now been opened up and you can drive through it to come out by the rear of the church at Mill Lane. On the land either side of the road exclusive houses and bungalows have been built and it is also proposed to build a children's play park and a new village hall here. On the left hand side of the main road we have a small estate called Wardens Close with bungalows which were originally built for the elderly but, as demand has dropped, have been let or sold.

Walking along the road we pass the automatic telephone exchange and three modern bungalows. The first one, where retired farmer John Tucker lives, was where the first village hall (Barton Hall) stood. The hall, opened in 1920, was named after Captain and Mrs Barton. It was a low, galvanized building which had been purchased from the Holy Trinity Church, Barnstaple, with money raised by concerts, fêtes and such like. The Barton family were the main organisers in these fund-raising events.

Betty Netherway (née Tapscott) was born and brought up at Wardens Hill opposite where Barton

Ariel View of High Bickington, 1988.

Archie Merrifield outside his blacksmith's shop in North Road, c.1920.

Brownscombes' Saddlers, c.1890.

View of Howards and North Road with Ellicott's the butchers on the left, 1925. (R.L.K.)

James Leythorne who had owned the Ebberley Arms Hotel and later lived at Doric House, North Road. He is seen here, c.1910, at The Strand, Barnstaple, where a horse sale was held during the week of Barnstaple Fair.

Left: *Wardens Hill, the house where Mr Dick Farley and the Tapscott family used to live.* (A.S.)

Below left: *The Meeting Point which was first built in 1834 as the Brethren Chapel. For several years up until the late 1800s there was a school here. The chapel was demolished and rebuilt in 1913. See the photograph of the hunt in North Road in Chapter 12 and note that the Brethren Chapel was rebuilt at a different angle.* (A.S.)

Above: *Jean Tapscott outside The Stables Health Centre (in 1988), built in 1979 on land where the stables of Eddie Owen's bakery had been.*

Left: *Loveham Farm, 2000.* (A.S.)

Above: *High Bickington young ladies waiting for the school bus. Left to right: Karen and Lucy Hedges, Sarah Jane Tanton, Becky Lock, Olivia Bowd and Laura Clarke, c.1993.* (R.L.)

Right: *Dawn Cottage and High Down in North Road, 2000.* (A.S.)

Hall stood. Her family lived with her maternal grandparents Mr and Mrs Richard Farley. Betty remembers the hall as the Reading Room for men only, and where they also played billiards and skittles. One of her grandfather's jobs was caretaker and she can remember him taking her to the hall where she tied dusters on her feet and skated up and down the skittle alley to dust it. She still remembers the smell of the chalk that lingered in the air as they cleaned the floor.

Wardens Hill Cottage stands on the corner of Pound Lane, which leads down the steep hillside and passes Stowford, Southbrook Stud, Loveham, Culverhouse and Broadwood, eventually joining the A377 road near Smallmarsh. On the opposite corner of Pound Lane are two cottages, Dawn Cottage and High Down. At the beginning of the 20th century there was just one house, and what is now Dawn Cottage was the store barn for the market garden that the owner, Jack Patt, ran in Pound Lane.

We now pass houses on both sides of North Road. On the right we have Town Farm where Mrs Betty Harpum, churchwarden and keen horsewoman, lives and where Mr and Mrs Fred Pidler used to live with their children Christine and John. Christine with her husband Cliff only live two doors away now. Postman Reg Wonnacott used to live next door and Jack Kent, a road contractor, was in the next house.

We then have what was Wonnacotts' Bakery at North Road Stores. Today Penny Povey runs a printing, photocopying and anything-to-do-with-computers business there. Her husband Ken is a designer and production engineer who works long into the night in a shed at the bottom of their garden. Next to their shop was the forge of blacksmiths Walter Dunn and, later, Archie Merrifield.

On the opposite side of the road we pass Doric House where Mr and Mrs James Leythorne lived. They had lived at The Ebberley Arms when their only daughter Primrose married Robert Underhill of Week Farm, Burrington. They later had a house called White Bridge built on the outskirts of the village where grandson Bill and his wife Joyce lived. Bill was a much loved and respected man of the community but died suddenly in 1999.

In the late 1800s North Road Farm used to be Brownscombes' Saddlers. Afterwards, it belonged to the Dunns, blacksmiths who also had petrol pumps and a shop which stocked tools and hardware goods as well as cigarettes and pipe tobacco.

Main picture: *Doris Towlson, Ken Gill and 'Ma' Gill outside The Golden Lion, c.1940.*
Top inset: *Mrs Nancy 'Ma' Gill, licensee of The Golden Lion, c.1950.* (R.L.K.)
Bottom inset: *Licensees Lesley and Richard Enfield outside The Golden Lion, 2000.* (A.S.)

Above and left:
*North Road,
late 1920s.
There is a
petrol pump
outside Dunns'*
*Hardware Shop. The barn on the left belonged to
Doric; the same scene in 2000.* (A.S.)

The Golden Lion comes next. From the records this appears to be the only building that has not changed in use. In *White's Devonshire* dated 1850 it is recorded that the licensee of the pub was Charles Brownscombe, maltster and victualler. Was this the same family who owned the saddlery next door? The Golden Lion remained in the Brownscombe family until 1889 when George Tucker became the maltster. In *Kelly's Directory* of 1893 John Cousins is listed as being in residence, as is John Hooper in 1906. In the past century, I believe, the best remembered licensee was Mrs Gill, known affectionately as 'Ma' Gill. Before moving to High Bickington she had lived in London and had been a psychiatric nurse and a policewoman, which certainly gave her the character and stamina to manage a country pub. Ken Gill, her son, was an insurance agent so her daughter-in-law Dorothy later took on the licence. Dot Gill, who was born in the village, still lives here with her daughter Barbara. Today The Golden Lion is run by Richard and Lesley Enfield.

Opposite The Golden Lion stands North Road Chapel on the corner of Bakers Street. This lane leads to the Stables Health Centre and on into the High Street. A few yards further up the main road we come across the hub of High Bickington's everyday life, High Bickington Stores (see chapter 5). Outside the shop is where the bus stops to take people to Barnstaple. The bus shelter opposite was built with a donation from Mrs Laura Woollacott who was a native of High Bickington but who lived in America for 60 years. When she returned for a visit she had been upset to see everyone, especially the children, standing in the rain while they waited for a bus.

We now reach a point on the main road where it branches back into the High Street and the centre of the village. Howards stands on this corner. This imposing double-fronted house with blue wooden shutters was bought by Bernard Cole (see Chapter 15) and it remained in his family until his granddaughter, Ruth Mardon, sold it in 1999. Alan Woodcock who lives at Kingford is in the process of restoring it. As the photographs show, part of this house was a shop and here one could buy china, haberdashery, coal and 'fat bacon'. To look at the house today it is difficult to imagine there being room to keep a few milking cows in a shippen at the rear of the property, and that later it was licensed as a slaughterhouse! I am assured of this by Bernard Cole's grandson Stan Tucker, who remembers having to deliver the meat around the village on a Friday night.

A few yards on we arrive at Stone Cottage which was the stables belonging to the largest house in the village where the gentry or clergy lived. Today the house is called The Old Rectory but it has also answered to High Bickington House, Holes and The Sycamores. However, whatever it has been called it has not changed in appearance since the earliest photograph I have seen, taken over 100 years ago.

With the pace of today's traffic it is not safe to linger in this narrow part of the road but on our right is a cottage called Valetta, where Miss Down and Miss Margaret King-Heal (as seen on the front cover of the book) lived. Miss King-Heal was known as 'Aunt Meg' and had been a lady's maid. She died in 1929 at the age of ninety. Next door is Myrtle Cottage, which for many years was Ellicotts the butchers.

We are now at Cross Park, no doubt named because it is a crossways. To our left is Shoplands Lane and to our right Back Lane. Following along the main road there are seven houses. The first six were built by Devon County Council, between 1948 and 1954, and the last by Devon and Cornwall Constabulary as their Police House in 1964. These houses are now all privately owned.

General Gardiner outside his home, The Sycamores, btn 1881–1896. The house was also known as High Bickington House, Holes and The Rectory.

BACK LANE

I cannot be sure if this is an official name for this road, as it is not on any map of the village. Perhaps it is just a local descriptive name – it does, after all, lead down the back of the village. However, I am informed by Mrs Kathleen Down who lives in the road that many years ago it was always called Pound Lane as there was a pound for stray cattle at the bottom. It was in Back Lane late one March night in 1929 that everyone of a certain age will remember where they were when the lane became the scene of a serious fire. It was Parsonage Farm that was ablaze and the conflagration was discovered by Rose Eastman (née Setherton), her sister Winnie and her future husband Jim Harris. I visited Rose at her home in Bishops Tawton and she clearly remembers the events of that night.

The group had been to a dance at High Bickington Church Hall, which Rose says was then called Wansbrough Hall. The two girls worked for the Reverend and Mrs Wansbrough at Beechwood House. The rector's wife was very strict and insisted they left the dance before the end to discourage 'followers' (little realising that such details were arranged long before the dance finished!). After the discovery of the fire Rose ran back to the hall and raised the alarm. Jim and Winnie set about letting the animals out before the people came from the dance. The farm belonged to John and Elizabeth Cole who lived there with their children Edgar, Nora and May and Mr Cole's Uncle Sam. Edgar, who now lives in the neighbouring village of Ashreigney, says he was only eight years old when the farm caught fire and all he remembers was being lifted from his bed and carried downstairs and across the road to stay the night with Miss Newbery, the school teacher.

Mrs Cole was the only one not in the house that night as she had been helping with the refreshments at the dance. Several people remember that Uncle Sam, who was disabled, could not see any good reason why he should leave the house! However, with a thatched roof to feed on the fire soon caught hold. Every available person in the village turned out to form a human chain with water buckets dipped in the stream at the bottom of the village and passed back to the fire.

As the blaze appeared to be threatening the cottage next door it was decided to evacuate. An elderly lady named Lizzie James lived here and Rose and Winnie went to great pains to persuade her to leave. She insisted she was not going without her pots of jam and her parrot, and she loudly proclaimed that she wanted to know the whereabouts of her 'best vest!' Not until the girls convinced her that they had it with them could they get Mrs James to vacate the building.

Rose remembers the dress that she wore that night. It was lemon taffeta and was completely ruined after the events of the evening. The girls arrived back at the Rectory at 3a.m., nervous at the reception they would receive from their employers. However, they need not have worried as they were treated as heroines. An earlier call on the telephone to the Wansbroughs ensured that they knew of the part the girls played in the night's drama.

Top: *Rose Setherton, c.1930, who was house-maid at the Rectory when she discovered the fire at Parsonage Farm.*

Above: *Rose Eastman (née Setherton) recounting her memories of her life at the Rectory in 2000.* (A.S.)

Left: *Bill Parker, 1984, outside Homewell with the pump that provided water for his family for most of their time at the cottage.*

Back Lane, c.1910. The 2nd person from left is Florrie Parker, 4th from the left is Horace Bartlett (the postmaster's son). The house in the foreground is where Elias and Eva Parker brought up their 15 children. The next cottage up is where Ned and Polly Parker lived and Walter and Ivy lived in the cottage on the corner.

Lower village with Homewell in the right foreground, 1920.

Main picture and above inset: *Parsonage Farm with its thatch roof before 1929 and after the fire in that year.*
Right: *After the fire John Cole surveys the fire damage at Parsonage with his daughters Nora and May.*

Walking on we pass the lane to Little Bickington Farm and Sammy Couch's cottage. The Couch family have lived here for over 100 years and a few years ago Sam had the building renovated after the cottage next door, where the Milford family had lived, had to be demolished.

Next door to Sammy, on the other side, is White Rose Cottage where Ned and Polly Parker lived. Ned's parents, Elias and Eva, had 15 children and lived in the adjacent house now called Lyndale. This later became White's, the wheelwrights and carpenters. Roger and Jennifer White live there still.

Opposite are two roads that skirt two thatched cottages and emerge in Poplar Terrace. However, before taking this route we will continue a little further down Back Lane. We pass Prospect House on our right and then the Methodist chapel which was built in 1834 by the Bible Christians. Across the road is Quarry Lane, so named because it led to a small quarry. On the corner is Steps Cottage where outside there is a sign which states 'Caution Free Range Children'. It is here that you realise how lucky we are

to live in this peaceful area where children can play in relative safety.

A few yards further on we come to the edge of the village with Lower Farm on the right and Homewell on the left where Bill Parker and his wife Lily lived all their married life. Bill was well known for his large kitchen garden from where, I am told, he supplied half the village with fresh vegetables and soft fruits. He was a very warm-hearted, generous man, although with his broad Devonshire dialect I could not always understand everything he was saying.

After Lil died Bill carried on living in the cottage but refused to have any modern conveniences installed – including electricity because he feared that it would set fire to his thatched roof! Only with a great deal of persuasion from friends in the village did he agree to have the cottage brought up to the standards of the 20th century. Unfortunately Bill was not well enough to continue living on his own and the house had to be sold. It has now been tastefully modernised and eagerly awaits its new owners' full-time occupation.

Hope Cottage, c.1920.

Farmer Joe Tucker from Deptford with his pony Jack outside Prospect House in Lower Village, c.1920. The house in the background is where Elias and Eva Parker brought up their 15 children.

JUNKET STREET

Entering Poplar Terrace from Back Lane between Prospect and the two thatched cottages called The Cottage and Rose Cottage we have Junket Street on our left. Could this have been so named because the long low house that dominates this lane used to be a dairy farm named Lower Farm, until its replacement was built? Victor and Violet Parker farmed from here and their son Stan and daughter Sylvia were also born on the premises. Sylvia and husband Dick Pidler still live here and Dick has carried out his carpentry and undertaking business for the past 40 years from the workshop attached to the house.

Opposite Junket Street is the cottage where Bunny Snell remembers spending the war years with her aunt Mrs Brownscombe, sister of her mother Mrs Mock. Bunny never left as she later married Gerald Snell and brought up their family here.

POPLAR TERRACE

Poplar Terrace is no doubt so named because it was once lined by poplar trees. On our left is the picture postcard, thatched Hope Cottage and on the right is the Old George Inn. I am told that about 150 years ago this was an old coaching inn.

However, 100 years ago this building was two cottages. The first was the residence of Walter Ham, the schoolmaster who rented from the owners Mr and Mrs William Newbery who lived in the rest of the building. Mrs Newbery was also a schoolteacher, as was her mother Mrs Bending and her daughter Bessie. Bill Newbery was a foreman carpenter who worked for the Pyncombe Estate, and was known as 'Friend' Newbery as he called everyone 'Friend'. No doubt he suffered, like a lot of us, from 'name blindness'!

In 1977 Michael and Jean Kellaher obtained permission to convert their home The Old George into a restaurant. After several applications to the Licensing Justices they were granted a licence to sell wines and spirits. Once again The Old George became a hostelry. There have been several licensees over the intervening years. In the 1980s it was Edward and Phil Eyres who already lived in the village and were popular members of the community. They later furthered their skills in catering by becoming part of the group that turned Libbaton Farm into a golfing complex. Most recently, Jenny and Jim Thomas, with the help of daughters Sarah Jane and Emma, provided hospitality in the 'old-world' atmosphere of the centuries-old building with natural oak beams and large open fire.

Adjoining the Old George Inn is Brewery Cottage, which is also thatched. I have found no evidence that this was a brewery but do know that it was in fact two cottages. In the 1891 census we find John Beer the blacksmith living here and, next door, Richard Bending the church clerk. In the summer these cottages have a 'chocolate-box' prettiness, with flower tubs and hanging baskets.

On the other side of the street are two houses with birds' names, The Jays and Swallow House. Susan Jay lives in the first house, hence the name. Charlie Brownscombe the wheelwright had his workshop between these two houses. Today it is incorporated in The Jays. Charlie lived next door at Swallows House which later became the home of Nurse Steer, the district nurse, known by everyone for miles around simply as 'Nurse'. She lived here with her aunt, Miss Evans.

Top left: *Dick Pidler, carpenter and undertaker, 1999.* (A.S.)

Top of this column: *Edward and Phil Eyres behind the bar of the Old George Inn, 1986.*

Above: *Jim and Jenny Thomas, 1998, licensees of the Old George at the turn of the century.* (A.S.)

Poplar Terrace, c.1890, with trees, looking towards The Black Horse public house. The workshop in the left foreground was Charlie Brownscombe's wheelwright's shop.

Main picture and inset: *Poplar Terrace, c.1910, with only one tree remaining. Dr Good's motor cycle is stood outside his surgery (now the Post Office); the inset picture shows the ground (on the right) which was the 'tye pit' where the Church Hall was built in 1925.*

THE MARKET HOUSE

The garden next door to Swallow House was the site of the market cross, which later became Market House. In the 13th and 14th centuries after a charter was granted to hold a weekly market a space had to be found to accommodate it. In most villages this was the church cross, its stepped base being used to set out the people's wares. As there is no evidence of a church cross at High Bickington we can assume that a market cross was built for that purpose. The Market House would have replaced the cross and been owned by the lord of the manor, who charged rents for the use of the space and stalls. This building was quite an advance in comfort from having to sit out in the open selling your butter and eggs.

In the 1822 edition of *Magna Britannia* it is recorded that the Market House was demolished 'within the memories of persons still living'. The Market House Inn was situated where the Post Office is today. In 1908 Dr Arnold Saxty Good lived here and started the first surgery High Bickington had ever had. It was a tailor's shop before William Bartlett opened it as the Post Office, which purpose it still serves today (*above*).

The Church Hall, c.1925, built on waste ground where old cottages once stood. The verandah is now enclosed.

THE CHURCH HALL

First built in 1925, by donation from the Revd and Mrs Wansbrough, the Church Hall stood on a rather wet and muddy piece of ground known as 'the tye pit' where it is thought a number of cottages had previously stood. The building was called Wansbrough Hall until 1937 when it was passed over to the Church Council and was renamed. It is not the most attractive building but it has been the centre of all the village activites since the Barton Hall closed.

It is here that functions such as fêtes, jumble sales, Parish Council meetings, Parliamentary voting, wedding, funeral and christening parties are held; and in the past dances, concerts and even post mortems and coroners inquests! Today it is also used as a nursery school and a meeting place for the Women's Institute, gardening and judo clubs and many more events including a get-together to discuss and gather information about this book.

MILL LANE

Leave Poplar Terrace, turn left and High Bickington Primary School appears before us with its playground at the side. Follow the road in front of the school and one arrives in Mill Lane, a very narrow lane which until recently was the only route leading out of the village to Lee Farms, North Heale, Yelland and on to Ebberley. Now the road through the housing estate eases the traffic burden.

Three old cottages are followed by three new houses, built on what was the edge of a field. The last old cottage is Lower Green Cottage where Mr and Mrs Patt lived with their sons, Jim, Owen and Alfred. Owen Patt's daughter, Freda Loosemore, who has worked alongside her husband Tom at Atherington Post Office for many years, can remember visiting her grandparents' cottage and finding chickens and other livestock in the kitchen. She recalls that the kitchen range 'smeeched' so much that quite often the smoke was so bad you could not see who you were talking to across the room! Mr and Mrs Alf Lemon lived in the middle cottage. Alf was a cobbler, sweetshop owner and part-time postman and is remembered for what the children called 'finger weight'. As the scales went down when he was weighing out the sweets he would quickly take the top one away. An observation by someone who was a child in those days was that she did not know how Mr Lemon would cope today with EEC hygine rules, as he went from mending dirty boots to serving sweets in one swift movement! Mill Cottage is the last in this row and was where smallholders Michael Squire and his son Bill lived.

Below: *Cottages in Mill Lane, 1999.* (A.S.)

Above: *Mill Lane, 1998. The Patts lived in the first cottage on the left. Cobbler and sweetshop owner Alf Lemon lived in the middle cottage and the last was owned by Michael and Bill Squire.*

Left: The *High Street after 1945 (c.1950) showing the church with its round clock face (and note the petrol sign at the end of the building that was Gooding's Store).*

Right: *Sam Naylor is standing outside his shoe repair shop, once the Commercial Hotel, with his two sons, late 1920s. The thatch was removed in 1930. The Post Office in the right hand foreground was Dr Good's surgery in the early 1900s. On the left was the Police House. The large stones on the corner were to stop the cartwheels scraping the walls.* (K.P.)

Left: *The author and her mother Mrs Barthram viewing Harris' Shop, c.1950, prior to moving to Devon from London.*

Right: *Poplar Terrace, c.1925, facing Eddie Owen's baker shop. The Church Hall had by this time been built at the top of the street. The cottages in the right foreground were later the Old George Inn.*

HIGH STREET

Returning to the High Street and standing with our backs to the school we are in the widest part of the street. This is where all of the parents park when collecting their children from school or when there is a function in the Church Hall. You can visit the library van here on every other Tuesday. This is also where the carnival queens used to be enthroned before their procession around the village.

On the left is pretty Kingsdown Cottage, where Mrs Rawle, known as Granny Rawle, lived with her four children – John the veterinary surgeon, Fred the slaughterman, Mary who did housework at Little Silver House and Georgie who was housekeeper for the Newberys at the Old George. Tim and Sally Webb live in Kingsdown Cottage today. Tim, a retired RAF Group Captain, is responsible for the organisation of the North Devon Show, a major agricultural show held for one day in August at Huntshaw Cross.

Tim Webb organising the annual North Devon Show, 2000. (A.S.)

A little cottage, which is now incorporated in Kingsdown, was where Miss Manning the Sunday-School teacher lived. The 1891 census tells us that Robert Cole, the butcher, lived here. Much later, James Mitchell had a butcher's shop in the front and a slaughterhouse at the back.

The next house is called The Old Bakery, although whenever it is referred to by local people it is called 'Betty Mitchells', because Mrs Mitchell lives here now and has done for 40 years. However, it has had many uses other than simply as a private dwelling. In 1850 it was The Black Horse run by Thomas Bealy, victualler (who in 1857 was also listed as a farmer, cattle dealer and tax collector – obviously there was not a good living in selling ale). The licence was transferred to Richard Coats in 1866 after the death of Thomas Bealy, but in a local newspaper dated 1870 the police were recorded as having objected to the renewal of the licence for Richard Coats, as there was recorded a conviction for keeping a disorderly house in the previous year and, prior to that, one for having deficient measures in his possession. The Customs and Excise men must have found High Bickington without too much trouble in those days.

In 1882 The Black Horse was the venue for the inquest on William Mounce, a farm labourer who worked for Mr Gill (perhaps the John Gill who lived at Little Bickington Farm). The deceased had been rolling a field with two horses pulling the rollers and was found 'quite dead' by Thomas Baker late in the afternoon. The body was conveyed to the schoolroom where William Alfred Norman, a surgeon from Torrington, carried out a post mortem at 10p.m. I will not dwell on the injuries but suffice to say Mr Mounce could not have been a pretty sight. A verdict of 'accidental death' was returned.

Between 1889 and 1893 the licence for this public house was held by Nathaniel Tucker who is recorded as a cattle dealer. After this time there is no further mention of The Black Horse. However, Mrs Audrey Norman, who lives in the village today, can remember a rhyme on the outside wall of the house, which must relate to the time when it was The Black Horse.

From saddle to tree
I'm thrown you see
Still clutching at the mane,
So stranger stop
And take a drop
To help me on again.

For a short period of time this building was the Post Office. The sub-postmaster William Bartlett, who was also a grocer and baker, then bought the house across the road (today's Post Office) and moved the Post Office with him. Mr Turner, Eddie Owen and then Mr Hockridge ran their bakery businesses from these premises, hence its present name. In 1962 James Mitchell and his son Peter bought the house and Betty and Peter brought up their three children here. But even then it was not the end of the working life of this house. High Bickington was in dire need of a doctor's surgery, so Betty's front rooms were pressed into service, as was Betty herself. She worked as the doctor's receptionist and general factotum for 34 years. Her rooms were High Bickington's health service for 17 years until the new surgery was built in 1979 on ground which had been stables at the back of Betty's home.

We arrive now in the narrow part of the High Street. On our right is the Post Office run by Lorraine and Tony Cummings. The Commercial Inn was next door in 1857 when William Down was the victualler. He was also a timber merchant. In 1949 Jean and Dick Tapscott began their married life here and raised six sons. Jean remembers that they rented two rooms (one up, one down) from the owners, Mr and Mrs Samuel Naylor. Sam Naylor was a cobbler and sold shoes and boots from what is now the front room. He was also a school governor and part-time postman. Syd Squire remembers an incident when he was a young lad playing in the High Street. Butcher Slee was passing the cobbler's shop when

View from Church tower towards the High Street, c.1925.

Sam Naylor was standing in the doorway. Mr Slee said, 'I don't fancy your boot laces are very tough' to which the cobbler replied, 'That's more that I can say about your beef!'

Jean and Dick later bought the Naylor's house and Carrie's Cottage, next door, which Jean thinks was once the servants' quarters of the Commercial Hotel as there was only a plaster-board partition between the two houses.

The rest of this side of the street is now taken up with private dwellings, but was once High Bickington's equivalent of a superstore. Henry Gooding senr, who was a tailor by trade, started in the grocery business in 1874. In *Whites Devonshire* of 1878 we find him listed as a grocer, tailor, draper and seedsman. He had four sons, Jack, Henry junr, Silas and William, who later carried on their father's business. Henry's only daughter married William Bartlett who had the grocery and baker's shop and then the Post Office. (An interesting fact, Henry senr's father served under the Duke of Wellington against Napoleon.). William married Mary Slee from Libbaton and had three children, Harold, Doris and Clifford, who carried on the business with his wife Gwen until they retired. Their daughter Jennifer now lives in a house which overlooks where three generations of her family provided for most of the needs of the parish.

Crossing over to the other side of the street opposite the Post Office we have the old Police House. This was the home and station for the resident Devon Constabulary policeman and his family until the new Police House was built at Cross Park in 1965. The next-door neighbours were Freda and Owen Patt – Owen was a rabbit trapper.

As we have already passed two houses in the High Street one might expect next to arrive at No. 3. Confusingly, it is No. 1 South View. It was here that Ern Pidler the carpenter lived after he married Beattie Way. Unfortunately they were only married a short time as Ern died of lead poisoning from the lead paint he used at work. Later Mr Harris lived here and built a smithy at the rear of the house, where it opens on to Bakers Street. No. 2 South View was in fact the first Post Office in the village. Mr and Mrs Lewis Snell moved here from Burrington, with their two eldest children. They later had another nine! Mrs Snell was the postmistress whilst Lewis was a water bailiff. They later moved to Prospect House and farmed land at Seckington. Mrs Snell lived to within three weeks of her 100th birthday and is remembered with great fondness in the village.

Lawn House comes next. Here in 1891 lived John Slee, butcher and farmer. Later a slaughterhouse was built at the rear of the property and in 1925 a butcher's shop was opened on to North Road. Today this is High Bickington Stores.

Noah Bird, stonemason, lived at Virginia House, and the last house at this end of the High Street was originally two houses. The first is a very unusual three-storey thatched house where Dave Pickard, a railwayman, lived. The other was the home of Mary Ann Snell whose husband had also worked on the railway.

Above: *View down the High Street. Note the girl with the bucket at the pump in The Square, c.1920.*
Bottom: *Rambler Cottage, 1999, in The Square. Dave Pickard the railwayman lived here.* (A.S.)

THE SQUARE

In The Square stands a pillar made of stones which I am told were surplus to requirements when the gateposts were built at Little Silver House. On top was placed an oil lamp, which was exceedingly useful at night when filling your bucket with water from the village pump which stood beneath it. Today the pump and the lamp have been removed and the only use the pillar has is to be hung with flower baskets in the summer. A Cattle Fair was held in The Square on the first Monday after 14 May – an event which heralded a week of festivities for the villagers. The custom was discontinued in the 1950s.

At the head of The Square is a house called Candar. A century ago Frederick Hooper, a horse dealer who owned The Ebberley Arms, lived here. The shop that now stands empty at the rear of the house was a manure store owned by a Mr May. Later it became a general store owned by Jim and Emily Harris (as seen on the front cover). This remained as a shop run by Mr Jim Lawson until the mid 1970s. His wife Ann, who still lives here, was the district midwife at South Molton for 19 years.

There remains now only one narrow lane to complete our walk around the village. This takes us from North Road, opposite The Old Rectory and between Myrtle Cottage and a high wall, behind which used to be the kitchen garden for The Old Rectory. Today the wall protects a bungalow from the elements and from the traffic that thunders through this narrow part of the main road. The high wall continues until it reaches Rectory Cottage which was obviously once Church

property. Mayfield Cottage comes next, which in its former life was a blacksmith's shop and then a slaughterhouse owned by Mr Ellicott the butcher. Retired builder Maurice Ridd has painful memories of when he was converting the slaughterhouse into the house it is today. He recalls the amount of time and back-breaking work it took to remove an old engine, which had run the sausage-making machine from the rear of the building!

The two garages that stood next to Mayfield have been removed and a large double-fronted house erected. The lane now becomes very narrow and although traffic can drive in both directions it is not advisable.

There are four cottages clustered together on our left before the lane opens up into Poplar Terrace, beside the Old George. Doreen Ridd has happy memories of her childhood in Rose Cottage. Her father George Heale was the village lamp lighter and lengthman, her mother Gertie was one of Elias and Eva Parker's 15 children. Gertie used to walk to the quarry at Shutely with Granny Short, who lived next door, to break stones for road making. All this, and she raised six children in a two-up, two-down cottage! The cottage next to Granny Short's was a shippen, which gave rise to the nickname for this lane. If you do not know what it is I shall have to leave you guessing!

COMING TO GREET YOU.

Colonel and Mrs Channer driving their Rally car with horses in tandem along the unmade road beside the River Taw, c.1900. This road was later to become the A377, the main road between Exeter and Barnstaple.

Charabanc outing to Bampton Horse Fair, 1913.
This photograph was taken outside The Bell Hotel. High Bickington people recognised in the vehicle on the right include Mr King (first man with the hat), next to him Bill Slee of Libbaton and the woman on the far right, Mrs Rippon of Deptford.

Chapter 4
Transport

ROADS

Before 1750 most goods in rural Devon were transported by pack horse along narrow paths, lanes between fields and riverside tracks. However, as wheeled vehicles became more common, so the need increased for an improvement of the roads.

The first mailcoach arrived in Barnstaple in 1827. Before that, a stagecoach travelled between London and Barnstaple three times a week. They journeyed by what was then the main road from Exeter, along the ridgeway of the hills above the Taw Valley. It came by way of Morchard Bishop, Chawleigh and Chulmleigh, branching off to South Molton and to Barnstaple. The Barnstaple route dropped down to cross the River Taw at Colleton, then up to Burrington, High Bickington, Atherington and Fishleigh. This would support the theory that the Old George Inn was a coaching house.

Above: *Col and Mrs Channer, c.1910 (with chauffeur Edwin Ellicott) - they owned the first car in High Bickington.* Below: *Kingford Bridge opening, 1908.*

In 1830 the Barnstaple Turnpike Trust built a new road in the floor of the valley from Fishleigh to Crediton, a distance of some 20 miles. By 1832, tollhouses had been built at Chapleton, Abbotsmarsh and Colleton Mills. Tolls varied from area to area depending on who owned the stretch of road and the width of the wheels of the vehicle. After the opening of the North Devon Railway from Exeter to Barnstaple on 12 July 1854 the toll system was no longer profitable for this length of road.

Before 1908 the only way to cross the river at Kingford was by way of a ford. A thick wire was stretched across the river between two trees to mark the line of the ford. This must have been useful for strangers to the area or at times when the river was running high. The Kingford Bridge was built by the Barnstaple firm of Woolaways and largely financed by local subscription. A big crowd of people gathered on the bridge for the grand opening ceremony which marked the opening up of trade and communication to both sides of the valley. And, not forgetting matters of a romantic nature, young men could now go courting without getting their feet wet!

With the arrival of the railway and the need for access to the stations along the line, the road at the bottom of the valley (now the A377) became more important than the ridge road through High Bickington. It was around the time of the First World War that this road was first metalled. Syd Squire, who was born just before the war, told me that his first job after leaving school was road making. He

View of Rose Cottage, Kingford, with the River Taw and Portsmouth Arms in the background, c.1900. This was taken before Kingford Bridge was built.

The River Taw flooding at Kingford, 1963.

Kingford Bridge under construction, 1907.

Kingford, c.1900, before the road was made up, with Rose Cottage on the left and Marwood Cottage on the right.

remembers that he had to start work at 6.30a.m. feeding and cleaning the horses. Then, after a breakfast of fried herrings, bacon and potatoes, he drove his horse and butt to wherever they were working.

Stone was taken from the local quarries (there being at least three in this parish at that time) then carted to stone depots by the roadside where they were cracked to the size of eggs – does anyone remember the 'stone cracker' that used to rumble and rattle away in the depot at Kingford? The roads were laid with stones, then mud was spread over them. The steamroller followed to flatten and compact the stone and mud. It was a thrill for Syd to be allowed to climb up with the engine driver to relieve him of the monotony of driving to and fro. Road making was a winter job because a great deal of water was required and Syd recalled that in those days there were no waterproofs and all he had for protection was a sack around his shoulders and others around his legs. All that for six shillings a week!

The first car to visit High Bickington was in 1903 on the day the red flag was abolished. It was a Benz driven by Augustus Greenwood-Penny and his brother Sidney, medical students at St George's Hospital, London, who were visiting their parents at Nethergrove. The journey took a fortnight, averaging 17 miles a day! As petrol was not widely available outside London they had to make do with paraffin. Another problem encountered was horses. They were petrified of motor vehicles so whenever the intrepid adventurers approached one the engine had to be switched off and it took 20 minutes to restart. This entailed the carburetor being drained, cleaned and topped up with a small amount of petrol, as the car would not start on paraffin.

The car only had two gears, forward and reverse, and many hills had to be climbed backwards. The roads were rough and stony and the car had solid tyres. I wonder if they sent a postcard along the route saying, 'Having a great time. Wish you were here!'

Colonel Channer who lived at The Sycamores was the first person to own a car in High Bickington. Then there was Doctor Good with his Fiat and Mr Aitkin of Nethergrove who had a Nazzaro. Later, tradesmen such as the general store's Goodings and the butchers Slee and Ellicott had delivery vans.

The first car-owners in the village had to buy petrol in two-gallon cans from the local shop, where it was stored in a concrete bunker. They would also purchase a spare can and strap it to the running board of their car. Later, there were two petrol pumps in the village. One was outside Dunn's Hardware Shop, which sold Shell. The other belonged to Goodings and had Pratts petrol; it stood in The Square at the end of their property. How ironic that today we have to travel about three miles to obtain this expensive commodity!

Top: *Dr Good on his rounds at Umberleigh Bridge in his 1910 single-seater Swift 7hp, 1915.*

Second from top: *Albert and John Eastman sitting in a Morgan Family three-wheeler at Shuteley, c.1925. Behind is a Rover 9/20 made between 1924-27.*

Third from top: *Dr Good with new Triumph, 1908.*

Above: *Goodings Model T Ford van by their petrol pump in The Square.*

RAILWAYS

The North Devon Railway, which ran from Exeter to Barnstaple, opened on Monday 31 July 1854. When the inaugural train arrived at Barnstaple Station there was a great deal of celebration. The directors of the North Devon Railway and Dock Company were met by the Mayor and Corporation, and the town's clerk Mr Bencraft read out a speech of congratulations. A procession led by a troop of the North Devon Mounted Rifles paraded around the principal streets of the town, which were spanned by triumphal arches and thronged with spectators. About 1000 people sat down to a lunch in the new Market Hall. The day's events were brought to a close with a ball for those of fashion and rank in the district.

Above: Howards, c.1910, the home of Bernard Cole. His daughter Annie is standing in the doorway - china is displayed in the shop window.
Below: Commemorative steam train on the Exeter to Barnstaple line at Kingford. (G.W.)

Although Barnstaple was awash with celebrations the villagers on both sides of the railway line must have been just as jubilant. Travel and communications became possible to a degree never known before. Not only could the locals travel to Barnstaple, Exeter and beyond, but also the whole area was now opened up to visitors. The souvenir business thrived. Crockery and decorative vases inscribed with 'A Present from High Bickington' filled local shops; Bernard Cole's shop at Howards, for example, had them in the window.

Life and work became a lot easier for most people. Milk, mail and newspapers were transported by train overnight. Freight trains carried heavy goods such as coal and timber. Drovers who had walked their sheep and cattle miles to the nearest market now only had to take them to the nearest station where there were cattle pens. Umberleigh had pens behind the platform and Portsmouth Arms had pens across the road in what was an old quarry. The animals would be auctioned here at a cattle market and then loaded into rail trucks and taken 'up country'. Sadly these cattle markets rang the death knell for the village markets and fairs.

Mail for High Bickington was now delivered by rail to Umberleigh Station instead of by road to Chulmleigh. Newspapers were also dropped off as the mail train went through on its way to Barnstaple. George Way, who was the signalman at Portsmouth Arms and also a newsagent, sold newspapers from Rose Cottage, Kingford.

Another of Syd Squire's vivid memories is of collecting coal from Portsmouth Arms Station by horse and cart. It was a long and arduous haul up Kingford Hill - two and a half miles and most of it steep. Portsmouth Arms was the station most used by people travelling to and from High Bickington, and in the mid-20th century had a staff of at least five. Today there are none and it is only a request stop. But at least we still have a train service, which is more than can be said for all of the former stations beyond the town of Barnstaple.

George Way, c.1930, the railway signalman who also ran a newsagency from his home at Rose Cottage, Kingford.

Railway staff at Portsmouth Arms Station, c.1920. Left to right: Reg Baker (porter), Mr Wheeler (Station Master), George Way, ?, Fred Southcombe.

BUS SERVICE

After the First World War cars began to make their appearance on the roads more often, although it was mainly the gentry who could afford them. People from High Bickington traditionally travelled to Barnstaple for their main shopping and for the market. As with other people in the Taw Valley and villages on the hills either side they would rely on the trains or the old-fashioned method of transport, horse and trap. If they went by train it was still a long walk up the hills back to the village, carrying their purchases. Even if they had a horse-drawn vehicle, quite often they had to alight to ease the strain on the poor old nag!

In 1920 William Parker from Burrington, who was a haulier, started the first motor-vehicle passenger service to Okehampton. Within a few years he was running a regular Friday trip to Barnstaple Market through High Bickington and Atherington. This was most welcome for the villagers as it meant they no longer had to traipse down the hill to Portsmouth Arms or Umberleigh to catch the train. Bill Parker also ran charabanc trips. High Bickington people could now organise Sunday-school, choir and bellringers' outings.

T. Heard and Son started another bus service in 1930 which ran twice daily from Chittlehampton through Chittlehamholt down the hill to Kingford and then up Kingford Hill. After travelling through High Bickington and Atherington it would return to the main road at Umberleigh and continue its journey to Barnstaple.

With the 1931 Road Traffic Act all bus services had to be licensed. William Parker decided to concentrate on his haulage business, which left Albert Turner continuing the Friday bus service through High Bickington. Soon after in 1932 Tom Wills of Chantry Garage, Atherington, started a bus service on Tuesdays and Fridays – Barnstaple market days. He had two buses in black and cream livery and the locals nicknamed them 'Atherington Magpies'. They ran along the ridge road from Burrington to High Bickington and Atherington, then downhill past Chantry Garage to the A377 at Fishleigh Rock and on to Barnstaple.

With a regular run to Barnstaple Market, farmers' wives could take their pannier baskets with their produce via the bus. This enabled the farmer to return to his chores rather than having to take the 'Missus' to town and wait until she was ready to return home. Tom Wills had a special roof rack fitted on top of his buses to transport all of this extra baggage. Can you imagine how long the journey took? The driver had to alight at every stop and climb up the back of the bus to load on these heavy baskets; and on wet days they had to be covered by a tarpaulin as well.

In 1937 children from High Bickington furthered their education after the age of 11 by going to school at Chulmleigh. They of course had to be transported there, and Tom Wills' buses were also used to this end. Gerald Snell, who had driven a delivery van for Goodings shop, obtained his HGV licence and did the school run twice a day. He also took the workmen to Winkleigh where they were building a runway for the aerodrome to be used for wartime planes.

During the 1940s and '50s there were still relatively few cars about and so Wills' buses did day trips and Sunday-school visits to the beaches such as Instow, Westward Ho! and Woolacombe. Mystery trips took in Lynton, Lynmouth and the beautiful scenery of Exmoor and always included a cream tea on the way home. Sometimes, depending on the clientele, the trip ended with a visit to a hostelry. There were also visits to pantomimes, fairs and carnivals at Barnstaple and Chulmleigh and to Bampton Horse Fair, as well as to Devon County Show, Bideford Regatta and Bristol Zoo. Later they became much more adventurous and did a weekend trip to see the Blackpool lights. Queen Elizabeth's Coronation on 2 June 1953 had every available bus in the county travelling to London to see the sights.

There was great difficulty in maintaining the bus service after the 1960s when there were more cars on the road. However, with the help of subsidies from the Rural District Council, the service to Barnstaple twice a week continued. After S.T. Wills' retirement Raymond Buse took on the business followed by Jim Pugsley. In latter years Terraneaus Tours of South Molton ran the twice-weekly service to Barnstaple from Chulmleigh.

In 1999, after a government initiative to persuade people to use public transport, we suddenly found that we had four buses a day, six days a week. These start at Exeter and travel through Chawleigh, Chulmleigh, Burrington, High Bickington, Atherington and on to Barnstaple. The return bus only goes as far as Chawleigh but returns to Exeter on the last journey of the day. Thus we are back to our historical past, on the old stagecoach route!

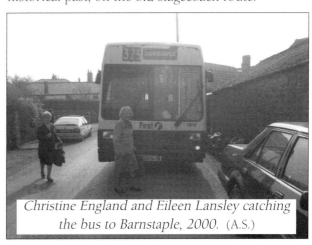

Christine England and Eileen Lansley catching the bus to Barnstaple, 2000. (A.S.)

An outing from the Golden Lion, c.1930. Mrs Lavinia Brownscombe was the licensee at the time.

*High Bickington choir outing, c.1920. Left to right, in bus: Harold Gooding, Bill Pidler, Bill Pester,
Bill Parker; in front: Albert Squire, Mr Ham, the Pidler twins - Essie and Gertie, Albert Squire junr,
Elsie Farley, Bessie Newbery, Elsie Squire, Mary Pidler, Mr Newbery, Ella Pidler, Mrs Pidler,
Lettie Tucker, Carrie Cole, Nellie Heales, Molly Snell, Revd Wansbrough, Amy Farley.*

Chapter 5
Trade and Industry

More than a century ago High Bickington was mainly self-sufficient. The roads and communications were poor and so the village people had to fend for their own needs and trade their goods and skills among their fellow parishioners.

In *Billing's Directory* of 1857 I found that High Bickington was listed as having four carpenters (William Heard was also a glazier), four shoemakers (Robert Payne, William Richards, William Turner and William Davey, who was also the parish clerk), two blacksmiths, four wheelwrights, two butchers and three shopkeepers (of these Robert Gill was also a farmer). There were two thatchers, one cooper, three stonemasons and a surgeon, Thomas Spencer, who also doubled up as the Registrar of Births and Deaths – well, at least both occupations had close associations!

W. Woolaway was a miller and there were four public houses – The Black Horse, the Golden Lion, The Ebberley Arms and The Commercial Hotel. It is understandable that with all the ale to be provided the village needed at least one cooper!

THE 1891 CENSUS

For the 1891 census a clerk walked the length and breadth of the parish, knocking on each door to gather and collate the necessary information. Most of the houses in the village did not have names or numbers. People were, therefore, listed simply as living in the village.

The census records for the first time that there was a police constable, William Mair, in the village. Ann Alford, who lived at High Down, was a nurse, but there was no longer a surgeon, although we did have a veterinary surgeon called John Rawle, and a lawyer, William Symonds.

The arrival of the railway shows its influence with four railwaymen in the parish. John Beer was the only blacksmith after more than 30 years of there having been two. Carpenters included John Hill, William Squire and George Pidler, who also earned his living as a wheelwright, as did James Taunton. Noah Bird, James Gooding and Robert Mayne were stonemasons and John Guard and George Lugg were 'lengthmen' or road contractors. To complete the manual trades there were 30 labourers, 17 of them agricultural workers.

Butchers included John Coats, Robert Cole, and John Slee. The grocers were Henry Gooding and William Heaman but there was no mention at that point of a baker. Obviously the ladies of the village were still baking their own bread.

The shoemakers in 1891 were William Turner, William Richards, who also ran the Post Office, and a William Henry Richards (perhaps the same person or father and son?). To complete the list we have James Kelly, a tailor, Margaret Turner, a dressmaker, and William Heale and Richard Morrish, who were grooms and gardeners. John Cole was gamekeeper to Mr Greenwood-Penny at Nethergrove and Mary Quick and Leticia Tucker were house-keepers.

Surprisingly, although there were several other large 'gentry' houses in and around the village, the census only lists two servants, Grace Page and William Sexton. Perhaps the others were not allowed to speak to the man completing the census form! Last, but by no means least, Richard Bending was the church clerk and the Reverend Yerbergh was the rector.

George Lugg worked for the Pyncombe Estate as a lengthman; he cleared the roads, ditches, ponds and quarries. He lodged with Lizzie James in Back Lane. Photo, 1906.
(Courtesy of the Beaford Archive)

Left: Syd Squire's family, 1914. Left to right: Sydney is on his mother's lap, sister Elsie, father Albert and eldest brother Albert.

Bottom: Bob Mellows, who had a newspaper round in the village for 42 years, catches up with the news with today's newsagent Guy Morton, 2000. (A.S.)

SYDNEY SQUIRE REMEMBERS TRADESMEN OF HIS CHILDHOOD

In many conversations with my neighbour Mr Sydney Squire my interest was captured by his memories of childhood, a number of which relate to the tradesmen of the parish.

Syd Squire was born in the village in 1913, the youngest child of Albert and Daisy. With his parents, an elder brother Albert and sister Elsie, he lived in part of Lower Farm where his mother was a dressmaker. They later moved to Hope Cottage and Syd's mother died when he was only six years old.

VISITING TRADESMEN There were still very few cars in the area when Syd was a lad and tradesmen sold their merchandise from the back of a horse and cart. One of them sported a bowler hat and blue bow tie with white spots and sold household utensils and china from the back of his canvas-covered, horse-drawn vehicle.

The Clovelly herring man would enter the village with his cry 'only a few left', and then 'fourteen a shilling'. He kept the herrings in a barrel, carried in a small cart pulled by a mule. The rag, bone and rabbit-skin man and the scissors grinder also made regular visits. Gerald Lewis was the rag and rabbit-skin man. He paid a penny for a pound of rags and a halfpenny for a rabbit skin. As rabbit was part of the staple diet (until the disease myxamatosis killed most of them in the early 1950s) there were always plenty of rabbit skins to sell.

NEWSPAPERS A Roborough man, Kit Harris, visited the village selling the *North Devon Herald* for 1d. He would carry the papers in a bag on his back and announce his arrival by ringing a handbell. Later, Mrs Snell who had run the Post Office, had the papers delivered direct from the publishers by rail to Umberleigh Station. Gerald her son then delivered them around the villages. Later his sister Lorna took over this job. In the 1930s she used to cycle to the railway station and collect the papers, then carried them, in bags over the handlebars and on a pannier, on the back of the bike. She cycled up the hill to Atherington where she did the first delivery, then on to High Bickington and finished at Burrington, returning home at about 4p.m.

After the Second World War, Bob Mellows, who had been a RAF Navigator, bought the round and continued to serve the villages in this area for 43 years. Bob has many happy memories of his time in High Bickington, including playing cricket and football with the children and the lemonade he had at Goodings Store. He also has fond memories of Roy Evans and Roy Blackmore, his two Saturday helpers. He recalls when they had a regular order for large hot pasties from the Golden Lion pub, and in the summer would sit in the hedge and eat them. Bob often helped the elderly with chores they could not manage themselves such as chopping wood and collecting several days' supply of water from a well, which was in the side of a bank. Today Guy Morton carries on the newspaper trade in the village.

Blacksmith Archie Merrifield attending to the elephant that was in the travelling circus sited at the bottom of Dobbs Hill, 1920s.

BAKERS Syd's earliest memory of a baker was a man who came from Barnstaple on Mondays, Wednesdays and Fridays. He travelled in a van pulled by a horse with an Army number stamped on its neck. (Farmers had to surrender some of their horses for the war effort and they did not always get the same ones back!). It was a long hard day for the roundsman who had little time to stop even for a meal so ate his lunch while travelling between villages – and his horse was treated in much the same way. As they entered the village the animal would have a round canvas nosebag with a wooden bottom put on and this was filled with corn, chaff and mangold (a type of swede). When they stopped, the horse would dip his head to the ground and have a feed. Very often the baker did not arrive at Syd's house until 7p.m., soaked through by the rain and still with nine miles to travel back to Barnstaple.

Later there were two bakers in the village who made their own bread. Mr William Wonnacott at North Road Stores used the old type of oven, which had to be fired up with faggots of wood, and the other baker Mr Turner, whose premises were once The Black Horse in the High Street, had a coke oven. Both did their baking in the morning and delivered the bread by horse and cart around the outlying countryside in the afternoon.

Mr Turner sold his business to Eddie Owen who was a baker and confectioner and who kept his oven going all day. Syd remembers seeing village ladies taking dishes of potatoes with slices of bacon on top to the bakehouse to get them cooked for their husbands' supper, a service for which the baker charged 1d.

Doreen Ridd, who has also lived all her life in High Bickington, has memories of working for Eddie Owen. She usually worked in the house but occasionally helped him on his delivery round. One day when they were taking a large order for a wedding reception and she was travelling in the back of the van with her friend Brenda Milton, Eddie took one of the bends in the road rather too fast and the back doors flew open shedding its load of bread, cakes and fancies, not to mention two extremely astonished ladies!

Above: *Horse and trap outside Goodings Store, 1915 - note the diamond-shaped clock on the tower.*

Above right: *Clifford Gooding with his delivery van, 1925 - note the telephone number.*

Left: *Betty, Dick and Jean Tapscott, 1942. They spent their early years in Grandfather Dick Farley's house, Wardens Hill.*

Above: *Graham Gooding outside his parent's shop in the High Street, 1936.*

Right: *Quarry Lane, 1962. Dick Tapscott is delivering for Goodings Store after heavy snow.*

Above: *Henry Gooding, who was a village tailor before opening Goodings Store in 1874. Photo, c.1880.*

GOODINGS Albert, Syd Squire's brother, served a four-year apprenticeship at Goodings as a grocer's assistant. During his first three years he did not receive any pay. However, his food was provided and for the last year he got two shillings a week. At work he wore a white coat with a white apron fastened round the waist. The grocer bought his goods in bulk so everything had to be cut, weighed and wrapped by hand. Very little string was used and of course there was no such thing as sellotape. Syd used to love watching the skill of his brother as he weighed and wrapped sugar, tea, flour, cheese, lard and meat while talking to the customers and barely looking at what he was doing. Sadly, Albert lost his life in Norway during the Second World War.

Goodings was the largest store for miles around and it sold almost everything anyone could expect to need. As well as food they had men's boots, ladies' shoes, socks, dress material, knitting wool, paraffin and oil, cartridges, oil lamps, sweets and a selection of medical and toiletry items – not forgetting the petrol from the pump in The Square.

A number of local people worked for Goodings over the years. Syd's wife Greta served behind the counter for many years. Betty Tapscott worked there before she married Fred Netherway. She did any job that needed to be done, then cycled around the district collecting orders and later making the deliveries. Her brother Dick also worked at Goodings as a delivery man. And so did Gerald Snell before he left to drive coaches for Tom Wills at Atherington.

The demise of the village shop came about as a result of the easier accessibility of the much larger town stores. With improved roads and transport people were attracted by the promise of cheaper products. Therefore, Goodings Store and many others throughout the country just could not compete.

Today's equivalent of Gooding's Store is North Road Stores owned by Richard and Margaret Gayton. The shop remained the butcher's from the time when John Slee opened it over 100 years ago, until it closed in March 1996. For a few months the village was without a general store. This made day-to-day living difficult and expensive when you had to drive at least three miles to buy a loaf of bread or pint of milk.

Richard had owned the milk round in the parish when he decided to take the gamble of buying and re-opening the shop. No doubt, with today's financial climate and the decline in village businesses, he was advised against such a precarious venture. However, it has proved to be a gamble that's paid off, especially for the people in the village, parish and the surrounding area. The shop is open seven days a week, from early morning until early evening and stocks everything from freshly-baked bread to bird nuts.

The village shop is not only where you buy your groceries; it is a central meeting point where people share their news and views and where messages are left. Some may call this gossip but it is what village life is made of. However, this venture has only been made possible by having faith in our community and a hardworking, friendly couple such as Richard and Margaret.

Top: *Mary Charity Gooding, c.1900, in Goodings Store which she ran with her husband William.*

Centre: *Gwen Gooding and daughter Jennifer behind the counter.* (Photo by James Ravilious and reproduced by kind permission of the Beaford Archive)

Bottom: *Richard and Margaret Gayton in High Bickington's Village Shop, 2000.* (A.S.)

BUTCHERS In the mid 1920s there were two butchers in the village, Reg Slee and Robbie Ellicott. Reg Slee had a butcher's shop in North Road where his father and grandfather before him had been in business. Both Robbie Ellicott and Reg Slee did their rounds with a horse and cart and they both did their own slaughtering. Later Robbie had a Model T Ford van and Syd used to help him on his country round. Syd was allowed to drive the van on these rounds but, as he points out, there was very little traffic on the roads in those days!

Iris Wicket, Robbie Ellicott's daughter, remembers that her father first did his slaughtering at Little Bickington Farm and then later, after he had opened his shop in North Road, he had his own slaughterhouse next to Rectory Cottage. A railway carrier came every week to collect the meat to go to Smithfield Market.

Now we come to a titillating tale for which I have no guarantee of authenticity. When he first left school young Bert Eastmond worked for Robbie Ellicott. A very eager and willing boy, he did every task 'on the run' and would be back on the double with, 'I've done that Mr Ellicott; what shall I do now Mr Ellicott?' This happened so frequently that Robbie got somewhat exasperated and one day he said 'Oh! go and stick your backside out of the bedroom window'. So off Bert went, soon returning with 'I've done that Mr Ellicott'. 'Cor, 'ave 'ee boy? Did anyone see 'ee?' 'Yes', replied Bert, 'And they said 'Good morning Mr Ellicott!'

Top right: *Greg Cannon, High Bickington's last butcher, 1992.*

Above: *Robert Ellicott opposite his shop in North Road, 1925.*

Left: *Myrtle Cottage, 2000 – once Ellicott's butcher's shop.*

WHEELWRIGHTS
Reginald White had a wheelwright's and carpenter's business sited in Back Lane which formed part of his father Bill's firm (in existence for many years in Atherington). It was here that Syd Squire was apprenticed and he remembers that he had to provide his own tools, so he bought two new saws at 12s.6d. each, a hatchet for five shillings and some second-hand tools from Charlie Brownscombe, a retired wheelwright in the village. Syd's pay was 7s.6d. a week and he supplemented this by working on farms in the evenings and at weekends.

W. White and Sons were classed as wheelwrights but did all kinds of agricultural work. They made horse-drawn vehicles for use on the farms, namely ladder carts which were mainly used during harvest time, and solid-sided butt carts which could be tipped up to discharge their contents, such as mangolds and dung. These carts were always painted blue with red wheels. When a farmer came to collect a new cart from the workshop it usually had the harness nicely cleaned and the brasses shining.

Syd always took great pride in his work when the horse pulled away with a cart he had just made.

Repairs formed a large part of their work and most of these were done just before harvest time. Farmers brought in wheels to be 'felloed' (pronounced vellied) which process entailed him assembling the six sections of the wheel rim and then the blacksmith Mr Fred Loosemore binding them. Syd told me that they would wait until they had a batch of wheels to do and then would spend a couple of days on the job. The blacksmith would be kept busy maintaining the fire at just the right temperature. When the metal rim was cherry red it was taken out of the fire and dropped over the wheel, and then cooled down immediately with buckets of water to make it shrink to a tight fit.

Although Syd was at White's in Atherington, whenever the workload demanded he was called to help at Reg White's in High Bickington and it was here that Dick Pidler (*above left*) and Keith Snell also learnt their trade. Dick went on to run a very successful carpentry and undertaking business from his workshop next to his house in Junket Street.

Syd's love and knowledge of wood is most evident when you watch him woodturning in the workshop in his garden. At 87 years of age he is still practising the arts and skills which he learnt all those years ago.

Above: *R. White (on the right) outside his father's wheelwright's and saw mills.*

Left: *Keith Snell and Dick Pidler outside Reg White's wheelwright's shop at High Bickington, 1950.*

Clockwise from top: *Dr Arnold Saxty Good with Rex his dog, outside his surgery in High Bickington, 1910; Dr Augustus Greenwood-Penny, 1904; District Nurse Margaret Squire who used to do relief duty at High Bickington, 1985; Nurse Stear doing her rounds on her BSA motorbike, early 1930s; District Nurse Sue Bickley getting down to her job in the treatment room of the surgery, 1999 (A.S.); Dr Richard Graham-Pole.*

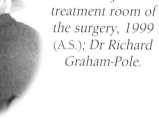

Chapter 6
Doctors in the Parish

The first mention of a High Bickington doctor which I have found appears in a newspaper dated 20 March 1837. Mr John Cocks, a Navy surgeon living in High Bickington, carried out a post mortem on 'an itinerant quack' who had been murdered outside The Ebberley Arms. Then, in December 1843, there was a notice in another newspaper of the sale of Mr John Cocks' household furniture and belongings, as he was leaving the district.

Dr Arnold Saxty Good

Dr Arnold Saxty Good was High Bickington's first general practitioner. In the early 1900s he rented rooms in the house that is now the Post Office, and from here he held his surgery. Mary Good, Arnold's eldest daughter, has given me a great deal of information about her parents.

Arnold was born in 1875, the third child of John and Fanny Good who both came from medical families. The boys in the Good family all have the prefix Saxty. Dr John Good died in India when Arnold

Above: *One of the families at Dobbs were the MacKays. Left to right: Moira, Nial, Dr MacKay, Mrs Kathleen MacKay, 1963.*
Below: *Dobbs in 1936. The barn on the left was the surgery and the other barn was where Dr Pole's daughter Jane can recall the barber coming to cut hair.*

was only eight years old. Being unwell, his mother was unable to look after her sons and it was decided to send them to a Dame School in Oxfordshire. Arnold and his brother Thomas did well and eventually trained as doctors at St George's Hospital in London, the same hospital at which their cousin Dr Augustus Greenwood-Penny of Nethergrove was trained.

After qualifying, Arnold worked as an assistant to a doctor in Chippenham. He then joined the P & O Line as a ship's surgeon. He loved his time at sea but after a while felt that he needed to settle down to something more permanent. Like his cousins, the Greenwood-Pennys, he loved the country and rural activities, he knew and loved High Bickington and there was a need for a doctor in the area as the nearest were in Torrington, Barnstaple and Chulmleigh. After a few years he bought the house called Dobbs just outside the village on the way to Barnstaple. The practice grew rapidly and because of Arnold's personality and reliability he

became a respected practitioner and loved friend of the community. He was a good obstetrician and was often called on by other doctors to help with difficult labours. Travelling gypsies came from miles around to have their babies delivered by him.

Arnold married Mary Gertrude Evelyn Crossing (Mollie) in 1913, at Berkley, near Frome in Somerset. Arnold had met Mollie when she visited her relatives Colonel and Mrs Barrett at Northcote Manor, Burrington. Four children were born, all at Dobbs: Mary in 1914, then John and Betty, and finally Robert in 1923.

Dr Good enjoyed being involved in village life and was a parish councillor, churchwarden and bell-ringer. He was a keen sportsman, loved to act and was good friends with Mrs Barton who staged many theatrical performances in the village. He was good with his hands and Mary still has a brass hot-water can her father made. He did his own car repairs if he could, and loved machinery. Arnold enjoyed speed and everyone knew the sound of his motorbike and the clouds of dust which heralded his approach!

Mary also recalls her father's love of thrillers and seeing him sitting for hours reading at the dining table by the light of an oil or petrol lamp, surrounded by his cigarette-rolling apparatus. Mary believes that it was his habit of smoking that was the cause of her father's death in 1931 when he was only 56 years old. Arnold became ill in 1930 and rapidly declined. He visited many specialists in London and went on a sea voyage to the West Indies. He died on his way home and was buried at sea - which is something he had often told his family he would like. When the news of the doctor's death reached the village it was received as a great shock and he was mourned by all who knew him. There is a brass tablet in the church commemorating him.

Mollie was 42 when she was left a widow with four young children to bring up. She sold the practice and Dobbs, which fetched £800 in 1931, and they lived at Bartridge House, Umberleigh. She continued to go to High Bickington Church, the Mother's Union and Women's Institute. She also ran the Sunday School at Umberleigh for many years. In 1963 she moved to Purley in Surrey to keep house for Mary who was a tutor at the Royal College of Nursing in London. In 1971 they both retired to Frome. Mollie loved to travel. At 72 she went to Uganda for three months to visit her sister Betty. She travelled to Canada about nine times, and celebrated her 95th birthday in Saskatchewan. She gardened until she was 103 and she was in bed for only one day before she died in 1993 aged 104.

Mary still visits High Bickington and has many friends in the area. I thank her for the fascinating story of her family and the doctor who is such a central part of High Bickington's history.

Mollie Good at the age of 100 in 1989, discarding her walking stick to clean the windows.
Inset: *Mollie in 1933.*

DOBBS RESIDENCE, 1936-45

Doctor Richard Graham-Pole (known simply as Dr Pole), his wife Doreen and their daughter Elizabeth arrived in High Bickington in 1936 to take over the general practice at Dobbs from a Dr Elwell. They were here through the war years and their three other children, Mary, Jane and John, were all born here. Jane has now returned to live in High Bickington, with Ian, her husband. John has followed in his father's medical footsteps and is now a professor in paediatric oncology in America. Elizabeth lives in Atlanta, America, with her husband and five children and Mary, who was a nurse and then a counsellor, is retired and lives in Harrogate, Yorkshire.

Along with the general practice Dr Pole was the police surgeon, carrying out post mortems for the coroner. He was also the 'poor law' doctor, an appointment under the Board of Guardians. This work entailed visiting the Workhouse once a week and if inmates needed medicine he had to submit a claim to the Board, which met weekly before it could be dispensed. He also had a weekly surgery at Winkleigh and with neighbouring doctors ran the cottage hospital at Torrington. He held his surgery at High Bickington once a day at 8a.m. and medicines were dispatched via the postman at 5p.m. each afternoon.

The garden at Dobbs provided all the fruit and vegetables the family needed during the lean war years. They also kept two pigs, poultry and ducks, as well as bees which produced 50 to 60lbs of honey a year. Dr Pole represented the North Devon Beekeepers Association and later became the Ministry of Agriculture Officer for research into acarine disease in the county.

Jane and her sisters remember their nurse, Nanny Phelps, and the ladies who helped their mother run the house. There was Nelly, the cook, two maids, Molly and Polly, and a cleaner called Iris. The gardener-cum-handyman was Roy Maynard who lived at Atherington. He had to pump up water from the well each day and during the war joined the RAF.

The Graham-Pole family left the village in 1945 and Dr Morris arrived. Sadly, this was not for long, as he committed suicide in the surgery. Dr Duncan followed, but after a short while left to join the Flying Doctor Service in Australia. The last doctor to have a practice at Dobbs was Dr McKay.

High Bickington was now without its own general practitioner, but Dr Carrier, who lived at Umberleigh, stepped into the breach and opened the surgery in Betty Mitchell's house. Several locums kept the practice going until doctor Harry Cramp from Torrington with his partners Drs Ben Armstrong, Malcolm Patterson and Rosemary Sheldon had the Stables Surgery built in 1979.

DISTRICT NURSES

Mention 'district nurse' in High Bickington and everyone says, 'You've heard of Nurse Stear, haven't you?' I did meet this well-known character once, when she was having lunch in the Old George Inn. She was then very frail but the air of authority was still evident.

'Nurse', as she was known, was not only the district nurse but also the district midwife. She arrived in High Bickington on 5 April 1927, when the area nursing association was first formed. She was a familiar sight on her rounds which covered the area from Torrington to the Taw and up as far as Dolton. This was a large area, especially as at first she only had a bicycle. Then after 18 months she had a motorbike. District nurses and midwives like Nurse Stear were very badly paid in those days and had to be on call 24 hours a day.

Inquiries about what she was like are met by women raising their hands and their eyes and saying with a laugh, 'Well, she was a very good nurse and certainly knew her job. But you had to do as you were told!' From this I assume that 'Nurse' was one of the old school and her word remained absolutely unquestioned.

Marion Stear spent all of her working life in High Bickington and stayed on well into her retirement. She was involved in most of the village activities and belonged to the Women's Institute. There are still many of Nurse Stear's 'babies' around to carry her memory into the 21st century. Today, confinements are usually made in hospital, but the nurses at the Stables Surgery cater well for expectant mums and babies.

Top left: *Dr Ben Armstrong sharing a joke with patient Reg Sussex at the Stables Surgery, 1999.* (A.S.)

Left: *Dr Good and spaniel Rex in 1910 outside his surgery (now the Post Office) with his motorbike and 1910 single-seater Swift 7hp car.*

Left: PC *Thomas Wonnacott (1848-1915) of the Devon Constabulary. He is seen here with his wife Mary. Standing behind are their children Frederick and William. Seated between her parents is Lilla Anne and at his father's knee is Reginald. In front is Stanley who was later killed in the First World War. The two eldest sons Archie and Ernest are not in the picture.*

Below: *Special Constables (left to right) Percy Bolt, George Harris, Bill Davis, Bert Shapland, Fred Andrew, c.1940.* (R.L.K.)

Right: *William and Albert Way who were both policemen in Cardiff.*

Below: *Police Constable Jenny Herniman, 1999. Off duty she rides a high-powered motor-bike.* (A.S.)

Left: *Special Police Constable Maurice Ridd on the day in 1992 when he received his long-service medal.*

Below: *Dave England (left), c.1980, who with his fellow officers John Stribley and Ruth Lawrence was awarded the Chief Constable's Commendation after disarming a knifeman threatening a baby.*

Chapter 7
The Boys in Blue

Time was when High Bickington had a 'bobby' of its own. Today, although we may have three police constables living in our village, the Police House that was also the Police Station last had a working life in 1970. It closed when a higher authority deemed that village policemen were no longer necessary. Just when the first resident policeman came to High Bickington is not clear, but here are a few snippets of law reporting from a local newspaper:

OCTOBER, 1863 Constable Smith investigated the theft of potatoes from a pile belonging to Mr Gooding of Loveham Farm. Footprints led to the suspect's dwelling where they found some potatoes 'like those stolen from the heap in the field!' The magistrates found the evidence circumstantial and dismissed the case.

AUGUST, 1864 James Pike was charged with leaving a horse and cart on a turnpike road. Constable Bending found the horse and cart and took it to the blacksmith's shop. John Jeffery the blacksmith said that after working on the horse it had wandered off. The defendant was fined 6d. with nine shillings expenses.

JANUARY 1867 A duck was reported missing by Thomas Bealey of Jump Farm (now Woodrow Farm). A suspect was seen passing through the village with a horse and cart at lunchtime. Constable Bending followed the man to Ilfracombe! The duck was found in the bottom of a sack (duck and sack were produced in court) in a stable at the inn where the defendant was staying. The accused was found guilty and sentenced to 14 days in the House of Correction.

SEPTEMBER 1869 Elias Woollacott of High Bickington was charged with stealing apples from an orchard belonging to Mr Harris, of Lee Barton. Mr Harris, having repeatedly lost apples, requested Constable Bending to keep watch. He did so one Sunday... and saw the defendant enter the orchard and take up one apple which the policeman took away, then ate it himself! The fine was 1 shilling and 9 shillings costs... paid by the boy's father.

Constable Bending was clearly a shining example in the art of detecting potato rustlers, duck snatchers and apple scrumpers!

APRIL 1895 John and William Pike were charged with being drunk and guilty of riotous behaviour. Constable Bending stated that on the evening of the 11th April 1895, he was sent for by the landlady of The Black Horse Inn, to turn the defendants out of the house. They refused to leave though they had a horse and cart outside. On getting them out of the public house a number of people surrounded them and wanted to fight.

The Revd Septimus Palmer spoke in their defence and told the court that there were not two more industrious young men in the parish. On the day in question they had been engaged in drawing manure for persons in the village. They had been treated to an unusual quantity of drink, which overcame them.

The Bench, taking into consideration the excellent character reference, fined them 1 shilling each and 8 shillings costs.

Perhaps on this occasion muck and money did not go together!

There is evidence that there was more than one policeman during this time in the village. On 21 June 1887 Constable John Garland wrote an essay for Mrs Gardiner who lived at The Sycamores, chronicling the day's events on Queen Victoria's Jubilee (see page 131). In the 1891 census William Mair is listed as a police constable.

Thomas Wonnacott (as seen in the photograph) joined the Devon Constabulary in 1876 and retired at High Bickington in 1902. His son William was later the baker who owned North Road Stores and his son Reginald was a postman in the village for 27 years.

On 31 March 1920, Constable Heales of High Bickington was presented with handsome cruet and cut-glass bottles to mark his retirement after 26 years' service. Mrs Heales received a case of tea knives in acknowledgement of the help she gave her husband in his extra duties during the war. After his retirement they moved a mile outside the village to Week Park where they had a smallholding.

Other constables I have heard mentioned are PC James (see the story of the lightning strike at North Heale Farm in Chapter 9). In 1939 there was PC French followed also by PC Swift, PC Fry and PC Mates.

PC 736 GUMM

Dave Gumm (*seen left, with Prince*) was the penultimate resident policeman for High Bickington. He still holds the village in great affection and all of the people he met here. He arrived on 1 June 1965 and moved into the new Police House with his wife, baby son Andrew and Dave's German shepherd Prince. The Police House in Cross Park also had an office, where the public could come for information, to make complaints and report lost and found items.

The beat was large and consisted of four parishes, including High Bickington, Atherington, Yarnscombe and Alverdiscott. This entire area was covered by bicycle, the furthest point being nine miles away.

PC Gumm could arrange what duties he worked, but he had to inform his superiors in Torrington, Bideford and Barnstaple two weeks in advance of the time he would be at any given location. Each point was near a telephone so he could be contacted with messages or notified of any incidents. Also supervisory officers could meet him and exchange paperwork (and of course check that he was doing his job properly).

With today's technology this procedure seems rather archaic. However, there was one occasion in 1966 when it worked well. Dave Gumm was cycling his beat between Umberleigh and Fishleigh Rock Garage where he was to make his point duty call. PC Dawe, who was on his motorbike on this stretch of road, informed Dave that he had had a message of a robbery at Instow Post Office. He gave Dave the registration number and description of the robbers' vehicle. Dave called at the garage and while here a car carrying two men pulled in for petrol. Although the car did not fit the description, when the two men saw Dave they pulled straight out of the garage without getting any fuel. Dave used the garage phone to call Barnstaple Police Station who contacted policemen on Umberleigh Bridge in time for them to block the vehicle. It crashed into the bridge and the occupants made off only to be soon found and arrested.

In the main Dave dealt with traffic offences but he also had to deal with barn and chimney fires, burglary and larceny of potatoes! Thefts of diesel fuel and petrol also cropped up, as well as that of a Burco boiler from Umberleigh Village Hall. Other crimes in a village policeman's remit included assaults and domestic violence, wilful damage, sheep worrying and salmon poaching. There were shotgun and firearms certificates to be issued at five shillings and renewed at 2s.6d. On 5 August 1967, the Animal Health Officer reported a suspected outbreak of foot and mouth disease. During this time licences were required by farmers to move cattle. They also had to use disinfectant at the entrances of farms for tyres and boots. Licences were issued at the police stations and there often had to be a police presence at the farm gates. This caused a heavy workload for the country policeman.

Until 1967 PC Gumm travelled his beat on a bicycle. However, after taking his test at Exeter, he became the proud owner of a 350cc Triumph motorbike. His beat became much larger taking in the areas of Beaford, Dolton, Petrockstowe, Monkleigh, Merton and Langtree.

Throughout the year there were many functions that had to be policed; events such as the Traction Engine Rally, Horwood Races and the May Fair at Torrington. There were also Umberleigh and High Bickington carnivals, dances and hunt balls. At many of these events a team of Special Constables assisted PC Gumm. He remembers Maurice Ridd (who went on to receive his long-service medal from the Chief Constable Sir John Evans) and Special Constables Farley, Congram, Webber and Ford.

Maurice Ridd recalls when Revd Plummer was their section sergeant and other 'Specials' were Tom Blackmore, Peter Pore and Diana Snell. Along with policing events they would have to train at Barnstaple and do a monthly duty with the regular policeman.

Dave Gumm left High Bickington for Ilfracombe on 20 March 1968 and was followed for only a short while by the village's last 'bobby' PC Graham Wilde.

OTHER PARTNERS IN CRIME

We cannot leave this chapter without mentioning other 'boys in blue' from High Bickington. There were brothers William and Albert Way, sons of Ellen and George Way of Rose Cottage, Kingford, who were policemen in Cardiff. We have David England, who served 30 years with the force. Dave had a varied and exciting career and is remembered for his part in rescuing a baby from a knifeman. Another 'home-grown' copper is John Tucker, son of farmers Stan and Eileen, who joined up straight from school at 16 and has been stationed at Exeter, Torquay, Plymouth and Camborne and is now the District Commander of Caradon and stationed at Liskeard. Last but not least is our 'lady in blue', Jennifer Herniman, who comes from Dorset but has been adopted as our own ever since she married farmer's son Derek. Jenny is now stationed at Torrington but lives in the village. Despite her demure smile and infectious laugh it would be wrong to underestimate this lady's abilities as she is a black belt, 3rd Dan in Aikido!

Chapter 8
Village Utilities

Water in High Bickington was a precious commodity until the mains were connected in 1952. Drinking water in the village was collected from either the pump in The Square or in the lower village opposite the chapel. There was also a pump outside the cottage called Homewell (which can be seen in the photograph on page 23). Some properties were lucky enough to have their own well, although the water still had to be pumped up by hand. Even Mr Wonnacott at North Road Stores had to collect all his water for baking from The Square.

The village's water came from an underground natural reservoir in North Road, just as you leave the village. During a rainless summer to avoid it running dry the pumps were locked by day and only two pitchers of water per household were allowed morning and evening.

There were no flush toilets or bathrooms. People had to bathe in front of the fire in a tin bath, and the toilet was the bucket type in an outside 'privvy'. This was emptied onto the garden and covered with ashes from the fire.

Electricity came to High Bickington very late. It was not until 1955 that the 240-volt mains supply was connected. The first payment for the Methodist chapel in December 1955 was 18s.2d. Before this time, lighting was by oil lamp or candle and heating by a Bodley stove which burnt either wood or coal. Flues had to be cleaned out once a week and stoves black leaded.

Astonishingly, prior to the First World War there had been street lighting by paraffin. During the conflict there was a blackout and the lamps were removed and not put back in peacetime. But although there were no lamps you could see your way around the village by the light from nearby houses. Cliff Gooding, who owned Goodings Store, had a generator which provided 110-volt electricity for his own use and also supplied other houses in his vicinity, including the Methodist chapel.

The postmaster's children, Bill, Percy and Gladys, c.1915. Bill used to ride a pony to Umberleigh to collect the mail from the railway station.

Eric Bolt remembers two fir trees being cut down to make electricity poles. He helped to remove their bark in the sawyard opposite the chapel and then painted them grey. Bill Parker dug the pits to stand them in, one on the corner by The Old George and one by Prospect House. A dedication service was held for the installation of the electricity on 12 September 1945. But it was to be a further ten years before the main supply was installed.

THE POST

Although the first mailcoach came to Barnstaple in 1827, the first mention I can find of mail to High Bickington is in 1850 when letters could be left with William Davey who was a shoemaker and a parish clerk. For the charge of 1d. letters would be delivered outside the village. In 1878 William Richards, a bootmaker, was also the postmaster. Letters came through Chulmleigh by mailcart. They were received at 8.15a.m. and dispatched at 5.15p.m. The nearest telegraph office was Umberleigh.

Lewis and Mary Ann Snell moved to 1, South View, High Bickington from Burrington in the early 1900s. Mrs Snell became postmistress and Lewis was a water bailiff. Dorothy Gill, Mrs Snell's daughter, told me that the postman used to bring the mail from Chulmleigh to High Bickington on horseback. He would then return to Chulmleigh and come back again in the afternoon. Mrs Snell thought that this was too much for one man, so arranged that he could stay in the village during the day, and while here he worked as a cobbler.

Later the post came by train and was left at Umberleigh Station. William Bartlett was then High Bickington's postmaster and his son William used to ride his pony to the station and collect the post in bags carried over the pony's withers. The return post went the same way. Once the post was sorted Sam Naylor delivered to the village and Fred Rawle,

Alf Lemon and Reg Wonnacott delivered around the rest of the parish. The time is still remembered by the older generation when you could post a letter to Exeter at 6a.m. and receive the answer by the last delivery at 5p.m.! You did, however, have to collect the letter yourself from the Post Office.

In 1921 William Bartlett moved the Post Office from the house that is now the Old Bakery, to where it still is today. This was later taken over by Mr Bull. Mrs Kathleen Down (Mary Ann Snell's daughter) started work for Mr Bull in 1926 and stayed with him for ten years. She then served as postmistress for the next 30 years.

During 1927 a telephone system was installed in the village. The Post Office staff and Mrs Down had to learn how to handle all of the plugs. There were very few telephones in the area but among those who had them were members of the gentry, the rector, and the doctor (whose number, I believe, was 8). The Police House also had a telephone. It has been described to me as one of those ones that was fixed to the wall where you had to turn the handle to connect to the exchange. Goodings Store's telephone was number 9 and it was painted on the side of their delivery van. Later the Post Office had a public phone.

Before telephones, telegrams were used to send urgent messages. Syd Squire often earned himself 6d. by delivering a telegram outside the village. During the Second World War, while her husband was in the Air Force, Freda Loosemore did a post round. She says that it was a long trip on a pushbike, especially one bad winter when the snow was deep and she had to go to Yelland Farm. She went up through the woods and the owls were hooting, but, she says, she was never afraid to be on her own. Quite often when she returned from her round there would be a telegram that needed delivering. After a hot cup of tea she'd be off again on her bike. However, she must have enjoyed the life as she has delivered the post at Atherington for over 40 years. With her husband Tom, who is the postmaster, they still run Atherington Post Office and this in the year they both celebrate their 80th birthdays.

Gerald Snell and his wife Bunny also played their part in keeping the Snell family tradition of the Royal Mail going. Bunny delivered telegrams around the farms and villages of Atherington, Yarnscombe and Burrington during the Second World War and Gerald became a full-time postman in 1950. At that time all of the post was sorted at Umberleigh Post Office, and Gerald, Frank Hookway and Harold Rice would alternate their rounds in Umberleigh and High Bickington. They also dispatched mail for Atherington, Burrington, Kingsnympton and Chittlehamholt.

Today the team of postmen includes Gordon Webber, Doone Baker, Barry Clemens, Graham Lake and Richard Lethbridge, each having their own specific round. Part-time posties, Brian Harper and Julie Woollacott assist them.

Richard Lethbridge's round is High Bickington. He is a well-known and popular personality in the area and has always got his camera with him to catch that special moment he sees when out around the lanes. He then mounts exhibitions and video shows for the people of the parish. In 1992 Richard won the 'Postman of the Year' for the South West. He then went to London for the finals where he became a runner up for the whole of the British Isles.

In spite of today's technology of e-mails and faxes Richard says people use the Royal Mail at an ever-increasing rate. The High Bickington round is the largest in the area and takes in 40 miles around farms and hamlets. With the new housing estates he has nearly 300 properties to deliver to. Many people now work from home, which of course increases the mail. And that's not forgetting all of the 'junk' mail, which has to be popped through letters boxes each day.

I must not finish this chapter without a last mention of our Post Office in the village. Today's postmistress is Lorraine Cummings, ably assisted on occasions by her husband Tony. In this era of centralisation village post offices are under threat of closure. It does not take a great deal of imagination to work out that this would bring intolerable hardship for a great many people living in the country.

Right: *Hazel Hedges in 1988 just in time for the last collection made by postman Richard Lethbridge (also a keen photographer of country life).* (A.S.)

Below: *Arranging the sweet shelf is High Bickington's postmistress Lorraine Cummings, 1998.* (A.S.)

Chapter 9
Farms Past and Present

At the turn of the last century farming was the main industry and the main employer. Now we find that the farmer often has to manage on his own and sometimes the farmer's partner has to go out to work elsewhere to bring in a regular income. Many of the younger generation do not want to carry on the struggle which their parents endure to earn a living and instead move away from the land that perhaps has been in their family for generations.

There were at least 40 farms in High Bickington parish a century ago. In the year 2000 there are just 14. As always, each day the sun rises and sets and the seasons arrive and depart. There is a time for the year-round tasks of ploughing, sowing, lambing, milking and harvesting, but there can be no dispute that agriculture has changed beyond all recognition. Today it is a more scientific affair with high-tech machinery and mountains of paperwork to contend with.

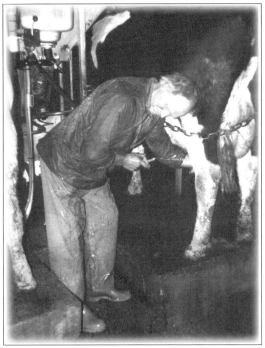

Stan Parker evening milking at Lower Farm, 1999. (A.S.)

Many local farms have been converted to other uses. One is a golf course and housing complex. Two are now stud farms. Another is a garden nursery, and another a cattery. Five have been made into groups of private dwellings and several have become holiday properties.

VILLAGE FARMS

North Road Farm has been in the hands of the Tuckers for four generations. It stands next to the Golden Lion and was once Brownscombes' Saddlers. The farmyard is at the rear of the building with open views over the valley and Exmoor. It is here that Stan and Eileen Tucker brought up their five children and where their youngest son Peter now farms with the help of his father. The farm is mainly beef, sheep and arable. Stan's grandfather started the farm with a few acres, which have been added to over the years.

Lower Farm is the home and workplace of Stan and Una Parker. With the help of Darren Ridd and Donald Baker they maintain a busy beef, sheep, arable and dairy farm. It was once Church property and the farmhouse was in Junket Street. When the council became the owners they built a new farmhouse on land at the edge of the village.

Peter Snell lives at Prospect House which his mother and father bought after owning High Bickington's first Post Office. Lewis Snell started farming at Seckington where Peter continues to farm today.

Town Farm is a farm no longer. It was the working farm of Frederick and Louisa Pidler and their children Christine and John (Louisa being the daughter of the butcher, William Slee). Today the small farmyard of Town Farm is used as stables whilst some of the remaining fields are a wildlife conservation area.

Little Bickington Farm is now a council-owned enterprise which is run by Dick and Evelyn Martin together with their son David. In 1888 it was occupied by William Hellyer who had moved from Winkleigh and stayed at Little Bickington Farm for 26 years. The newspaper report of his death noted that he was a popular man with a generous disposition and kindly manner. He was a founder member of the National School and occupied a prominent position on the Parish Council. His tenancy was to expire on the next Lady Day as Devon County Council had purchased the farm from the Pyncombe trustees and were going to divide it into smallholdings. Obviously this did not happen. With the tenancy now nearly complete, the Council has put forward an innovative scheme allowing the parishioners to utilise the farm for their own chosen project.

Left: *Sheep dipping at Dadlands Farm. Herbert Pidler is in the centre.*

Below: *Tom Goss of Vaulterhill Farm.* (T.G.)

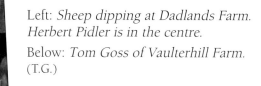

Left: *Don Baker moving the springtime lambs at the bottom of Braggs Hill, 1994.* (R.L.)

Right: *Times have not changed in some respects – Stan and Una Parker and Darren Ridd potato picking, 1999.* (A.S.)

Below: *The farming Tucker family outside North Road Farm, 2000. Left to right: Jeremy, Stan, Patrick, Peter.* (A.S.)

Bottom right: *Tom Miller with one of his many home-bred horses.*

THE PYNCOMBE ESTATE

The principal land-owner other than the Church was the Pyncombe Estate. The Pyncombe family had lived at North Molton and owned considerable property and estates in Devon and Somerset. The last surviving member of the family was Gertrude Pyncombe who died in 1730 and left all her property to be administered by a charitable trust for the benefit of the poor. (*See the photograph of the inscription on her memorial stone, page 63*).

The Pyncombe Charity Trust decided to liquidate all of their assets in High Bickington and an auction was held at the village school at 2p.m. on Wednesday 26 November 1919. As can be seen from the 'Schedule of Sale', most of the properties and lands were sold to the sitting tenants. It is also interesting to see that all of the dwellings and 1137 acres only realised £23 890. Compare that to the price tag of £240 000 for one house on our new village estate!

Over the next few years there was a change of ownership of the estate farms with only Yelland and Lee Farms remaining in the same families. Yelland Farm is today in the hands of Alan and Patricia Woollacott. Their son Simon is at college in Oxford, studying carpentry. Alan's parents Jim and Greta now live in one of the farm cottages nearby and his sister Marilyn lives just outside the parish boundary where she runs a mixed farm with her husband Steve Milton.

The farmhouse and barns are built in a quadrangle around the farmyard, an ideal design for a property that is so exposed to the west winds that prevail in our area. In Jim's day this was a thriving all-round farm with cattle, sheep, pigs and arable crops. With the changing atmosphere of farming, Alan and Patricia have given over half the farmhouse as a holiday let and they are converting some of the barns into stables which they will rent out. Alan is contracted to make and deliver haylage (horse feed) and Pat has a full-time job in Barnstaple. They still have an arable farm with cows and a few sheep, but regret that they have had to lose their prize-winning flock of Bleu du Maine sheep.

All around you is evidence of when Yelland was a hive of farming activity. In the enclosed yard outside the kitchen are the old pig houses and, screwed into the kitchen ceiling, are rows of black iron hooks where the hams were hung to cure. Marilyn

Above: *Binding before stooking during corn harvest at Parsonage Farm, 1915.*

remembers all of the procedures of producing ham and bacon, from the pig at the back door to the slice of streaky on the breakfast plate!

Lee Farm stands on the hill directly opposite its twin, Yelland, across a steep-sided valley. As the crow flies it is a short distance between the two farms; however, if you are walking it is a long, knee-crunching descent and a breath-taking climb up the other side. Jimmy Tucker farms Lee and, coincidentally, his brother Richard is his immediate neighbour in Lee Barton, just yards away. Richard works the farm with his wife Glenda Tucker and their son Andrew who lives a few fields away, at Heale Town Farm, which was his parents' first home and today accommodates a herd of 250 cattle.

Lee Barton was not part of the Pyncombe Estate but in 1878 it belonged to a James Harris. From 1889 until 1906 it was in the ownership of Richard Jones and then William Jones. A great-grandson, Jim Ward, now lives at Old Park. In 1923 another Eli Harris bought the farm, and two of his sons and a daughter lived here until Richard and Glenda bought it in 1995.

The farmhouse is thought to date back to the 1500s but was rebuilt in 1634 with further alterations in 1770. The exterior is imposing with landscaped gardens and spectacular views towards Exmoor and along the Taw Valley almost to Barnstaple.

The interior of the house meanwhile is a mix of ancient and modern. The kitchen is large and cosy yet modern and functional. When you go into the dining room you step back into the 17th century. Dividing this room and the hall is an oak plank screen. In the hall a plaster frieze bears a motif of prancing horses. The sitting room, which was the original parlour, has a fireplace with plaster chimneypiece and a glorious ceiling with floral motifs including a pair of plaster-cased crossbeams. This was the work of the Abbot brothers of Frithlestock.

When showing me this room Glenda told me about the ghost which is reputed to haunt the barton. One evening when she and Richard had settled down to watch television Glenda said she felt uneasy and could not relax. She felt as if she was 'being prodded to get up' – so she did and decided to busy herself in the kitchen. No sooner had she left the room than half the plasterwork ceiling crashed down on the settee she had just vacated. She feels that her

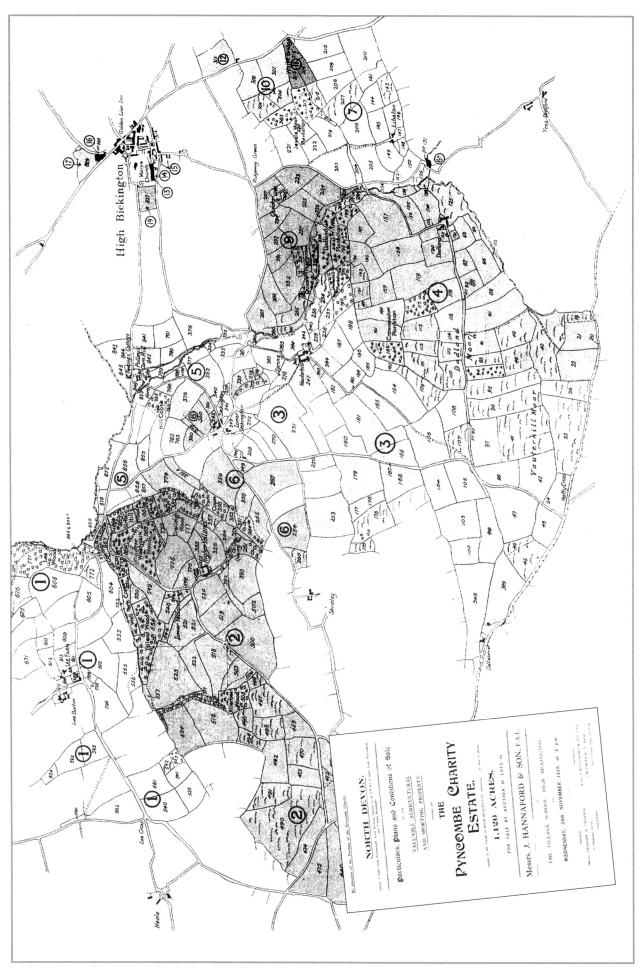

friendly ghost was warning her of the impending disaster. Mind you, it did not warn them how much it would cost to repair!

The ceiling had to be restored to its original condition as the whole farm has a preservation order on it and any alteration or building has to be carried out under strict guidelines. The Tuckers are experiencing the complexities of converting two old barns into holiday homes. There has also been an independent sighting of the lady ghost. Glenda and Richard were entertaining friends to an evening meal and the next morning the gentleman visitor told Glenda that while sitting at the dining table he had seen a little old lady in a long coat walk past the kitchen door towards the back door. Glenda says she is not frightened as she feels the old lady is a friend.

*General Charity—***Pyncombe.**

A.
96,571.

*Authority to sell real estate
(Auction).*

CHARITY COMMISSION

In the Matter of the PYNCOMBE CHARITY, regulated by a Scheme of the High Court of Chancery of the 5th July 1856 and comprised in a Determination Order made by the Charity Commissioners on the 23rd October 1906 under the Board of Education Act, 1899, s. 2 (2); and

In the Matter of "The Charitable Trusts Acts, 1853 to 1914."

The Board of Charity Commissioners for England and Wales, being satisfied by the representations of the Trustees of the above-mentioned Charity, and by a report from Charles John Hannaford, of Chulmleigh, in the County of Devon, Land Surveyor, that it will be advantageous to the Charity that the sale of the land and hereditaments described in the Schedule hereto, belonging to the Charity, and lately offered by the Trustees, with the approval of the said Board, at a sale by public auction, should be effected upon the terms hereinafter mentioned :

Do, upon the application of the Trustees, **hereby Order** as follows :—

1. The Trustees, within twelve calendar months from the date of this Order, may sell the said land and hereditaments for not less than the sums mentioned in the Schedule hereto, being the highest prices offered for the same at the said sale, and may do and execute all proper acts and assurances for carrying the sale into effect :

2. "The Official Trustee of Charity Lands," in whom the legal estate in the said land and hereditaments is vested in trust for the Charity, shall concur in the conveyance thereof if his concurrence is required :

3. The purchase moneys shall be immediately paid by the Trustees to the Banking Account, at the Bank of England, of "The Official Trustees of Charitable Funds" :

4. The proper expenses of the Trustees of the Charity attending the sale of the said land and hereditaments, upon an account being submitted by them to and approved by the said Board, shall be provided out of the purchase moneys :

5. The purchase moneys when so paid as aforesaid, or the balance thereof after payment of the said expenses when so approved as aforesaid, shall be invested by the said Official Trustees, in

C 3004 (2)

MEMORIAL STONE TO GERTRUDE PYNCOMBE IN POUGHILL CHURCH NEAR CREDITON. (A.S.)

IT READS: Gertrude Pyncombe of this Parish, Spinster, who was born April 9th and died March 19th 1730. She bequeathed her ample Property to uphold the dearest interests of human society By the better maintenance of the Religion among Men on the Knowledge and Practice of which depend the present and eternal Welfare of Mankind. Her estates of Welsbere Barton and others in the Parishes of Ilfracombe, High Bickington, Atherington, Idsley, Chulmleigh, Chawley, Burrington, Cruwys Morchard, Bishops Morchard, Oakford, Broadwoodkelly, Withypool and Ringsash in this County, and Dunster in the County of Somerset, are vested in Three Trustees forever, in order that the income may be applied to the Relief of the Poor, to the instruction of the Ignorant, and to the assistance of the Clergy in enabling them to augment all small livings, by claiming the Bounty of Queen Ann. In memory of the exemplary Beneficence and pious Zeal for the Church of Christ, this Stone is with all due Regard erected by the Trustees of her Bequests, JAMES BERNARD Esq. of Crowcombe Court Somersetshire. Rev., JAMES CAMPLIN A.M. Rector of Stoodley in this County and of Florey in the County of Somerset in the Year of our Lord 1809.

SCHEDULE.

The following freehold property, situate in the Parish of High Bickington, in the County of Devon :—

Lot No.	Description	Tenant	Acreage. A.	Purchase Money. £
1	Lee Farm	Representatives of Mr. Wm. Tucker and in hand	116·404	3,425
2	Yelland	Mr. J. H. Woollacott and in hand	235·242	3,375
3	Vauterhill	Mr. T. Goss and in hand	283·940	4,070
4	Dadlands	Mr. R. G. Pidler and in hand	170·996	2,330
5	Pulley Mills	Mr. Wm. Pidler	62·486	2,310
6	Part Seckington	Mr. W. Pidler and Mr. T. Goss and in hand	50·804	1,483
6a	Waste	In hand	·100	1
7	Libbaton	Messrs. T. and W. B. Slee and in hand	79·477	1,503
8	Witherhill	Mr. G. Pidler and in hand	47·099	1,593
9	Quicks	Mr. W. B. Slee and in hand	49·864	1,350
10	Jewell's Moors	Mr. G. Pidler	13·790	410
11	Whitebridge	Mr. Jno. Down	4·331	230
12	Jumps Close	Mr. Wm. Tucker	4·313	230
13	Cottage	Mr. Wm. Moore	·319	165
14	Pow's Cottage	Mr. Jno. Lang	·169	90
15	Estate Yard	In hand	·106	150
16	Cottage	Mr. W. Pidler	·287	145
17	Arable Field	Mr. W. Pidler	2·260	150
18	Warren's Marsh	Mr. R. G. Pidler	13·452	710
19	Little Barton	Mr. W. B. Slee	2·125	170
		TOTAL	A. 1,137·564	£23,890

Sealed by Order of the Board this 12th day of March 1920.

Above left and left: *The auctioneers' programme of the sale of the Pyncombe Charity Estate held on 26 November 1919 and the table of freehold property sold at the auction.*

Left:
Threshing at Pulley Mills, 1920. On the left is William Pidler; on the right is Sam Parkhouse who lived at Homewell.

Below:
William Pidler at Pulley Mills, 1920.

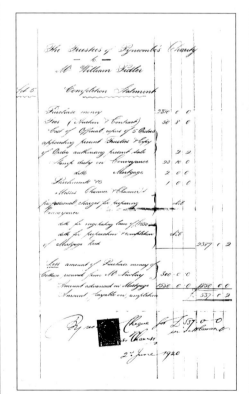

Above: *William Pidler's completion statement when he purchased Pulley Mills, 1920 (now Mill Brook) at the Pyncombe Estate auction.*

She just wishes she would give a hand with the washing up sometimes!

Glenda not only helps out on the farm but also does all of the office work. She recalls her father, who was also a farmer, telling her that when he started out all his paperwork was kept behind a vase on the mantleshelf. Now you need an office complete with computers, calculators and filing cabinets.

Vaulterhill was another farm on the Pyncombe Estate. Today it is a stud farm owned by Graham and Lynn Heal. In 1857 Mary Alford was the farmer here, followed by John Cowman and then William Chugg. Simon Goss farmed in 1901 followed by his son Tom who bought it at the estate auction.

Dadlands is named after Doda the farmer who was one of the first Saxons to inhabit High Bickington. In recent years it belonged to Robert Gill Pidler who bought it from the estate. Robert was married to Ada Blackmore, the grandniece of R.D. Blackmore, who wrote *Lorna Doone*. Their son Herbert married Doris Gooding, daughter of William Gooding of Goodings Store. Today Myc and Jenny Riggulsford live at Dadlands from where they run their public relations consultancy.

Pulley Mills, a water-driven corn mill, was bought by William Pidler (*see the bill of sale on page 64*). William's father Richard had been the tenant before him. Incidentally, Richard's wife was Mary Gill Blackmore, a niece of R.D. Blackmore. This makes the famous author the great-great-uncle of Dick Pidler who lives in the village today. William sold the mill at auction at the Golden Lion in May, 1931. Perhaps we could have a village sign that reads 'R.D. Blackmore was not here but his relatives certainly are'!

Witherhill was another farm owned by the Pyncombe trustees. It was purchased at the auction by George Pidler and later worked by his son William. The last people to farm here were George and Hazel Keen and it is now five separate dwellings.

Seckington was probably a hamlet and I have been told that there was once an alehouse here and definitely a school. There was also a water grist mill at Lower Seckington.

In 1825 an Admiral Bury died leaving his property of (Bale's) Ash and Seckington to his daughter Penelope. However, she could not dispose of it until after her mother's death. Likewise her mother could not sell the properties without Penelope's permission. The following year Penelope married Parson Jack Russell of Swimbridge, famous for the Jack Russell terrier breed. In accordance with the laws at the time Penelope's inheritance became her husband's property by marriage. On 10 December 1827 Russell wrote in his diary, 'Drove to Chulmleigh and transacted business with Gould, signed the deeds for the sale of Ash etc.' It is well known that Jack Russell was a keen hunting man and therefore it is reasonable to surmise that the properties of Bale's Ash and Seckington were sold to finance his passion for the sport.

In 1889 *Kelly's Directory* states that Francis Baring Short Esq. JP of Bickham Kenn, was the owner. He died in 1899 and his trustees administered his estate for many years. Another auction in 1920 shows the owner as Mr Tom Goss who also owned Vaulterhill Farm. It is interesting to see that one of the lots for sale was a 'Mazzard Orchard'.

Today Seckington is five separate dwellings with excellent views of the surrounding countryside and the village. Derek and Rosemary Munson live in one of the barn conversions and it is here that the remains of a roundhouse can be found. It had a big vertical post, with horizontal arms to which the horses were hitched. On top of the post was a cogwheel, which drove a shaft running through the barn. The horses kept walking round and provided the power for whatever was needed. This could be grinding corn or even running a dynamo to produce electricity.

Libbaton is now a golf course. Thomas Slee and his son William purchased the farm at the Pyncombe auction and it then passed to Mr and Mrs Corbett in 1947 and subsequently was sold to Elam and Maud Herniman in 1960. The Hernimans farmed Libbaton until the late 1980s. When Elam retired his eldest son Gerald, along with friends Edward Eyres and Jack Brough, decided to transform the farm into a golf course and a small housing complex.

Top and above: *Lee Barton, 2000, and the plaster ceiling and chimney breast in the lounge.* (A.S.)

Left: *Yelland Farm, 2000.* (A.S.)

Below: *Plucking geese, 1997. The lady with her back to the camera is Dorothy Milton. Facing the camera on the left is Greta Woolcatt and on the right is Marilyn Milton (née Wollacott of Yelland Farm).* (R.L.)

Below left: *Greta and Jim Woollacott outside Yelland Cottage, 2000.* (A.S.)

Left: *Iron hooks in the ceiling of Yelland Farm kitchen, 2000. These were used for hanging hams while they dried.* (A.S.)

Above: *Three generations of farming Woollacotts of Yelland, 1997. At the back of the quad bike is Alan, in the middle, his son Simon and in front is grandfather Jim.* (R.L.)

Right: *Lee Farm, Yelland's twin, 2000.* (A.S.)

Above right: *Libbaton Farmhouse, 1987.*

Above: *Harvesting oats at Libbaton, 1965. This is now the driving range at the golf course.*

Right: *Libbaton House, 2000.*

Above, left: *Part of the housing complex built at Libbaton, 1995.*

Above: *Geoff Stevens and Gerald Herniman laying the turf for the new golf course at Libbaton, 1980.*

Left: *Where there were once cattle, sheep and crops there are now the coiffured greens of a golf course, 1998.*

Above right: *Bill Pidler with small friend apple picking at home, Witherhill, c.1940.*

Above: *Witherhill Farm from the air, 1938. The property has now been divided up into several separate dwellings.*

Above: *Seckington Farm, 2000.* (A.S.)

Left: *The remains of a roundhouse makes a sheltered garden for a cottage at Seckington, 2000.* (A.S.)

NORTH HEALE

The most westerly corner of the parish once had several working farms. One remaining is **Heale Town Farm**. Others are **Old South Heale**, which is now Hidden Valley Nursery specialising in rare plants and owned by Peter and Linda Linley. **Hoopers Farm** (*right*) has now been converted into holiday homes but in 1891 was the farm of Henry Squire.

Commons Farm is a small sheep farm and **North Heale Farm** is the home of Dave Ginns who also owns the Golden Lion. Martin and Jenny Page live next door in Barnfield House. Martin was Managing Director of a London advertising agency but decided to escape the rat race and retire early. They intend to open their home to visitors for B&B and both also have a passion for big fast motorbikes (*right*). They each have a Harley and Martin has a Ducati.

In August 1933 an event described in the local newspaper as 'sensational and distressing' occurred at **North Heale Farm**. Mr Anthony Clarke was the farmer and his two sons James, 12, and William, 7, were about to start milking the cows when a bolt of lightning (described as resembling a huge fireball) hit the barn leaving one cow killed outright and both boys unconscious. James was so severely burned that Dr Elwell of High Bickington decided he could not be moved to hospital. A thatched barn, the milking shed and ricks of hay and corn were all ablaze and because of the lightning strike the telephone was out of order. However, with the help of neighbours and PC James and then the fire brigade, the fire was brought under control.

Dr Elwell wrote an article for the *British Medical Journal* describing how James Clarke, against all expectations, had lived and recovered almost all movement in his limbs. James had been carrying a galvanized bucket through which the lightning had earthed. One third of his body was terribly burned and in most cases this would have been expected to be fatal. Dr Elwell wrote that contrary to all medical expectations the lad made an almost complete recovery in ten months and in time would become a useful agricultural worker. I am pleased to report that James is still alive and well and lives in Torrington. Other farms which are no more include **Southwood** (*third from top, opposite*), now several separate dwellings, **Jump** (now Woodrow Farm), **Stowford**, **Broadwood** (*opposite*), **Culverhouse** and **Loveham**.

Higher Loveham is now Harbrook Stud, where Brian Harper (*top this column*) breeds Cleveland Bays. Monks bred these magnificent horses in the 1300s for heavy work and later crossbred them to produce the Yorkshire coach horses that pulled Royal Mail coaches.

Top: *Hoopers today is holiday cottages but used to be farmed by Henry Squire.* (A.S.)

Second from top: *Penny and Martin Page on their Harley Davidsons outside their home, Barnfield House, 2000.* (A.S.)

Third from top: *Southwood.* (A.S.)

Bottom: *Lower Broadwood, 1988.*

Opposite column, top: *Brian Harper with Wansdale Casper (Cassie).* (A.S.)

*Dudley and Elias Squire at Shuteley, outside Mowstead where the
ricks were made (as seen in the background), 1925.*

*Maud Eastman and her four sons, George, Albert, John and Bernard with Mary and Jack Cooke on a
ladder cart at Shuteley, c.1920.*

Bales Ash was one of the oldest farms in the parish; part of the building dates back to Norman times. Today it is the home of Jeremy Dawes and his wife Ines who runs a cattery and the RSPCA Rescue and Re-homing Centre from there (*opposite*).

Gratleigh was first mentioned in 1322 but in more recent years we find John Webber was the farmer in 1857. When he died the farm was offered at auction as a property ideal for a capitalist or a gentleman fond of fishing (no mention of farming!). In 1891 Edward Heal was in residence. In 1942 David and Mary Parsons bought Gratleigh and farmed it for 14 years. The description when it was then put up for sale stated that along with the 83 acres of dairy and stock farm there was a soundly built house with four bedrooms, a scullery with sink and a wash house with built-in copper – luxury indeed. Bert Parsons, who was born at the farm in 1948, remembers as a little boy helping out with his brothers and sister at potato picking and harvest time.

Shuteley has, within living memory, been two farms. In the 1891 census James Eastmond and John Turner were named as the farmers. In 1906 William Harris was in occupation and in 1916 Eli Harris of Weirmarsh Farm had a notice in the local newspaper 'to let by tender the farm of Shuteley'. In the 1920s Albert Eastman and Elias Squire were farmers here. Today four separate homes share this old farmstead.

Shuteley Cottage was one of the two farmhouses and was probably built in the mid- to the late-17th century. It is most quaint and when you walk in the front door it takes no imagination to step back in time. The living room was probably the only main room when it was first built and has a low ceiling with beams. A fireplace with bread oven fills the whole of one end of the room. The 3ft-thick cob walls and small windows may restrict daylight but keep the house warm in winter and cool in summer. The stairs leave the main room in the far corner and lead to the bedrooms right under the roof, which was once thatched. A step down from the main room is another room that dates back to the late-17th or early-18th century. This may have originally been the cowshed for wintering the beasts. Here there is another large walk-in fireplace and like most I've seen in old houses in the area it is well preserved. The heat of the oven has long been extinguished and the smells of the cooking and baking lost. I do not regret the invention of central heating but still remember the warmth and smells with nostalgia.

In the wall dividing the two rooms is an old cream hob (*opposite, second from top*) that looks

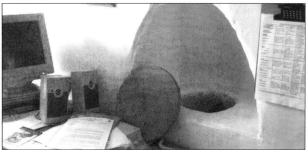

Top: *Ines Dawes takes charge of a stray cat from ambulance driver Diana Lewis at Bales Ash Cattery (also a RSPCA re-homing centre), 2000.* (A.S.)

Second from top: *A creamer built into the wall of Shuteley Cottage, 2000. Hot coals would be laid in the bottom of the hole and a bowl of milk sat on top. As the cream formed on the surface it would be skimmed off.* (A.S.)

Third from top: *Jane and Liam Bunclarke with daughter Hebe outside Shuteley Cottage, 2000.* (A.S.)

Bottom: *Jack Down at Deptford.* (R.L.)

Opposite column, top: *Twins Steven and Graham Down who farm Deptford Farms.*

71

Hedge laying and ditching demonstration, in a field belonging to Georgie Beer, c.1935.
Left to right: ?, ?, Mr King, ?, Bill Goss (in front of obscured unknown figure behind), Dick Farley
(the instructor), Harry Squire (with West of England corn sack around his shoulders), Dick Wythe,
George Eastman, Harold Eastman, ?, Lewis Squire, Walter Clatworthy and Bill Eastman.
Note – they are all using the Devon shovel.

Reed Combing at High Bickington, 1950s. Left to right: Colin Miller, Bill Underhill, Bill Parker,
Ernie Kingdom. (Courtesy of Western Morning News)

A class of the Dairy School held to teach how to make such things as cheese, butter and cream, c.1928. Left to right, back: Irene King, Freda Squire, May Miller, ?, Ruth Mardon, Billy King, Revd Wansbrough, ?, Laura Baker, Elsie Squire, Mary Bolt, John Tucker; front: ?, ?, Mrs J. Baker, Mary Blackmore, the two instructors, Gladys Tucker, Doris Tucker, Mrs Milton, Mary Laramy, ?.

Stella Burrows at Welcombe with her pride and joy, the rare herd of pedigree Sussex cattle. (A.S.)

Above: *Taking a lunch break while potato picking at Gratleigh, 1950.*

Left: *Preparing the ground for tilling at Gratleigh, 1945.*

out of place among the office equipment around it. Ella Boles (née Squires), who was born and brought up here, remembers the cream hob being discovered when they were decorating. Today, Liam and Jane Bunclarke live here. Liam, a chartered surveyor, works from home so that he can look after baby daughter Hebe while Jane works as a teacher at a local school.

Brothers Steven and Graham Down run the two **Deptford Farms** with the help of their father John. A short way up the hill from these farms was another called **Great Deptford**. It was here that Tom and May Miller farmed for 30 years with their son Colin. I visited Tom and May at their new bungalow at Seckington where they told me of their early days at Deptford. May said that it was an extremely hard life with no farmhands to help them. There was no electricity and water came into the house by gravitation. There were no tractors, only horses – they had three Shires and one eventing horse.

May had to work with Tom in the fields when help was needed and when Colin was a baby they would take him out with them and leave their dog Bruce to guard the pram. One day they were alerted by Bruce constantly barking and on investigation found that the pram had completely turned over, no injury having been caused to its precious contents!

As they did not have a car May would go to the village on a bicycle with Colin perched on the crossbar. There were only two buses a week and she usually went to Barnstaple Market on Fridays. One winter morning when May was going to catch the bus Tom shouted out to her to bring him back a newspaper. There was no newspaper delivery then and so they rarely had one.

May went off to Barnstaple and like most women from the country had a long list of shopping and errands to do before catching the return bus. It was not until she arrived home and was preparing the tea of herrings which had been neatly wrapped in newspaper (as they were sold then) that she remembered Tom's request for his own paper; she left the herrings' wrapping on the kitchen table, neatly folded. Tom came in and had his tea and really enjoyed this treat of fresh herrings. He then settled down with the paper. He read it front to back and not until he came to a photograph of people bathing in the sea did he realise that he had spent the whole evening with a newspaper at least five months old! May says that if he had never seen that photograph he would have been quite content with the news he'd just read!

Son Colin Miller and his wife had a new farm built in 1963 on the Ebberley road. Helped by son Paul they work this farm and do contracting work.

John Mulvey, the bronze sculptor, and his wife were later residents of Great Deptford and completely renovated the property. John's career and reputation took off in leaps and bounds during the 17 years they were in High Bickington and today he lives and works at Bickleigh, near Tiverton. Another enduring farm is **Weirmarsh** which belonged to the Fortesque Estates and was rebuilt when the arrival of the railway meant the original farm had to be demolished. Today, Peter May and his family run a large dairy, sheep and potato farm, their nearest neighbour up the hill opposite being **Berries Ground**, owned by Nicholas May. Still further up the hillside is **Snape** where Peter and Alys Hedges farm.

Last but not least is our only lady farmer, Stella Burrows, who lives with husband Ken at **Welcombe Farm** on the parish boundary with Atherington. It was built in 1922 by stonemason Noah Bird for his daughter Ella and her husband John Down on their marriage.

The earliest mention of Welcombe appears on 25 April 1882 when an auction was held to sell the freehold tenement comprising 16 acres, 0 rods and 20 perches of good pasture land and 2 acres of watered meadow. At the same auction Dobbs, which stands almost opposite, was offered for sale. Stella is proud of her herd of pedigree Sussex cattle but finds it very difficult to survive these times with just her farming. She teaches home economics at Chulmleigh School and belongs to WI Markets, a co-operative that sells home produce in Barnstaple Market every Friday. With all of the office work she has to deal with, like most other farmers, this lady's work is never done.

Chapter 10
School Days

During the mid- to late-19th century there were three schools in High Bickington; the National School and the schools attached to the Zion Chapel and Brethren Chapel in North Road. However, it has had only one since the 20th century, High Bickington Church of England School.

The school dates back to 1857 but the building was there long before, and it is thought that it may have been the Parish Poor House or Alms House or even where the clergy lived. We do know that in 1857 the building was altered to provide a place where children could take lessons.

THE PYNCOMBE CHARITY TRUST

In her will of 1730, Gertrude Pyncombe left her estate to be administered by three trustees. They were charged with managing the income from her property for the relief of the poor and the instruction of the ignorant, and the assistance of the clergy.

Under a scheme of the Court of Chancery of 5 July 1856, the Pyncombe Charity paid £50 yearly to a schoolmaster and schoolmistress for the two schools at High Bickington (remember the Brethren Chapel School?), the money to be spent on the instruction of reading, writing and arithmetic for the boys and knitting and sewing for the girls, and religious instruction for both.

Today, 270 years on, High Bickington pupils are still in receipt of the Pyncombe Charity Trust Fund. Each child who leaves the school at the age of 11 receives a small sum of money for the purchase of school books.

SCHOOL LOGBOOKS

School logbooks started in 1874 and were kept every day. The subjects taught were the three basics; reading, writing and arithmetic, with a strong influence from the Church in religious instruction. It is obvious from these books that the rector attended the school every day and taught the children. The Revd Langdon was the rector at this time and he appears to have had very close dealings with the education and the management of the school.

It was not compulsory for children to attend school until 1877, so when the weather was good and

School cricket team, 1929.
Left to right, standing: Alfie Harris, Harold Eastman, Kitchener Kent, Frank Rawle, Fred Squire, John Tucker, Tommy Davis; seated: Tom Goss, R.W. Pitman (schoolmaster), Willoughby Eastman, Sam Naylor (school governor), Tom Wonnacott; on ground: Jim Woollacott and Fred Lemon.

there was work be done on the farm the children missed school. On 24 July 1864 the schoolmaster Jack Orchard wrote that as the weather was fine several farmers had kept their children home to help with harvesting. The average attendance for the week was 55. Many of the farming seasons were noted in the logbooks, such as picking up potatoes, haymaking, apple picking, ploughing, sowing and harvesting.

Fridays were also noted for their drop in attendance. This was due to Barnstaple Market when the farming families all went to town.

Torrington Fair and High Bickington Cattle Fair, on the first Monday after 14 May, would mean few or no children at school. Eventually the school was closed for this event – as it also was for Ascension Day, the Annual Club and the Female Club (walks of the Friendly Society). Holidays were the 'gift' of the rector and he seems to have been very benevolent in this way!

There is much evidence of ill health in these early years. On 9 October 1874 the schoolmaster wrote, 'The cough is prevalent in this place'. There are also comments on throat diseases. Typhoid fever kept the teacher Miss Colwill from attending school on 3 November 1875. On 4 November 1878 the Revd

Headmaster Walter Ham (middle of front row), c.1881. He looks young here so this photograph was probably taken when he first came to High Bickington in 1881. The girl in the centre of the back row is Letitia Tucker who later became a teacher at the school and remained there until 1934.

This school photo was taken c.1890 in the churchyard. Mr Ham is on the left and Letitia Tucker (by now a teacher) is on the right.

High Bickington schoolgirls, c.1930. Left to right, back row: Miss Newbery, Phyllis Eastman, Edith Guard, ? Eastman, May Marshall, ?, Mary Bolt, Evelyn Sussex, Mary Eastman, Freda Squire, Miss Tucker; 3rd row: Freda Patt, Nora Baker, Brenda Clatworthy, Florrie Wonnacott, Irene King, Nora Norman, Mary Clatworthy, Nora Cole , ?, Irene Guard; 2nd row: Evelyn Smith, ?, ?, ?, Edith Heale, ?, ?, ?; kneeling in front: ?, May Cole, ?.

High Bickington schoolboys, c.1930. Left to right, back row: Tom Davy, Tom Goss, Harold Turner, Frank Rawle, Fred Squire, Kitchener Kent, Fred Lemon, headteacher R.W. Pitman; 3rd row: ?, ?, Edgar Cole, Alfie Harris, Harold Eastman, Tom Wonnacott, John Tucker, Willoughby Eastman, Stan Tucker, Alfie Short, John Eastman; 2nd row: Jimmy Woollacott, Percy Guard, ?, Donald Wythe, Jim Parker, Steve Tucker, Bert Guard; front: John Snell, Reggie Parker, Cecil Gooding, Cecil Brownscombe, Joe Tucker, Jim Harris.

Langdon told the master to close the school as the majority of children were absent with measles and whooping cough. The school was either closed or had only a few pupils until 31 January 1879. Henry Pearce the schoolmaster wrote that when children did attend they were too ill to study.

There are several reminders in these logbooks of the fragile health of children in those days, when you read, for example, quite matter-of-fact statements that a pupil had died or that the elder children of the school went to one of their contemporaries' funerals.

In those early years there seems to have been a problem with keeping teachers. After the Christmas holiday, the Revd Langdon wrote, 'The schoolmaster Mr J. Orchard being appointed to the governorship of the Honiton Union left this school unexpectantly at Christmas 1874'. The rector then had to take all the classes himself with the help of Miss Emma Mallett.

On 1 February 1875 John Carpenter became schoolmaster, but on 23 April he wrote, 'I resign the mastership of this school'. On 28 April 1875 Thomas B. Ashplant took charge with Miss Eliza Colwill as sewing mistress. He wrote:

The children are decent and generally well behaved. Miss Colwill reported the sewing and knitting very much backward. Lower class backward in writing and arithmetic.

By 24 December 1875 Mr Ashplant and Miss Colwill had resigned and George Luxton and his wife had taken over the role of teachers. Mr Luxton seems to have been more popular than his predecessor as the attendance numbers rose again and he notes that the discipline and cleanliness was improving. However, he had to caution some of the pupils for coming in late and for throwing stones during the dinner hour. They were also cautioned for 'insulting hawkers in the village', swearing at lunchtime and sliding up and down the road outside the Golden Lion.

Within 18 months the headship had changed again. This time Mr Henry Pearce wrote on 29 June 1877 that he had examined the school and found the pupils in the 'most wretched condition'. Their knowledge of geography and grammar were scanty. He had been obliged to deviate from the timetable, as it was impossible to work it. The Revd Langdon had visited every day and helped with the teaching.

On 8 October 1877, the children were informed that in future attendance at school would be compulsory and no child would leave before 12 in the morning and 4.15p.m. in the afternoon. By 19 October, numbers had increased to 82 (the most they had ever been) and on 26 October the rector told the master to inform the children that those over 11 years of age would have to pay a fee of 3d. a week in future.

From this point on there are many notes about the paying of these fees, which appear not to have been forthcoming on a regular basis! On one occasion H.F. Codd Esq., Her Majesty's Inspector, ordered that all defaulters' children be sent home to collect the money owed. On another occasion the schoolmaster wrote that to make up the register he had been obliged to advance the children's pence himself.

The attendance officer carried out his job with fortitude. A local newspaper report shows that parents at High Bickington were called before the magistrates to answer for the absence of their children. They all seemed to be of the opinion that the schoolmaster had made out his attendance returns incorrectly!

MEMORIES OF HEADTEACHERS

In 1881 Mr Walter Ham became the schoolmaster, and here at last was a man with staying power. He did not leave until he retired in 1925. We are now within living memory of a few High Bickington residents. Mr Ham was a bachelor who lodged with Miss Newbery at the lower part of what is now the Old George Inn. Syd Squire remembers Mr Ham well. He was known (no doubt secretly) as 'Slasher' Ham. He dressed in knee breeches and stockings, with lace-up boots, a butterfly collar with bow tie, and a flat cap. He used to cut a stick from the hedge to use as a cane which Syd assures me left it's mark both mentally and physically! Hence the nickname 'Slasher'. Nora Maynard (née Hellyer), the youngest daughter of Stephen Hellyer of Little Bickington Farm, has fonder memories of Mr Ham. She remembers him as a kindly man and a thoroughly good teacher, but when he was vexed he had a way of grinding his teeth.

Other teachers of this time who devoted their lives to the education of High Bickington children were Miss Newbery, whose mother and grandmother Mrs Bending had also been teachers at the school, and Letitia Tucker who was herself a former pupil and went on to become a qualified teacher. In 1934, due to a drop in pupil numbers, she left the school after 31 years to take up a new post at Atherington. Both these teachers organised the Sunday School for many years and played a large part in village activities.

More vivid memories of Syd Squire are of the coalman who brought half a ton of coal and emptied it into a pit under a trap door in their classroom. It was an honour to be chosen as the boy who went down into the pit to fill the coalscuttle.

Jim Westacott was the school attendance officer and he paid frequent visits to the school. When children had been absent for a day or two Mr Westacott was soon inquiring as to the reason. Families were often large in those days and at one time there were 127 pupils at the school so it was quite a task.

Then there were the doctor and dentist who visited the school. The pupils were all measured, examined and then weighed on a pair of spring balances hung on a large hook in the school doorway. The dentist carried out extractions and fillings in one room while the lessons went on in another.

There were no school meals in the 1920s and children who lived in the village went home for their dinner. However, the children who lived too far to walk home for a meal carried their lunch in dinner bags, which they hung along with the coats and hats on rows of hooks in the school porch. Unless the weather was really bad food was eaten out in the playground and a bucket of drinking water and mug were supplied for those who did not bring their own.

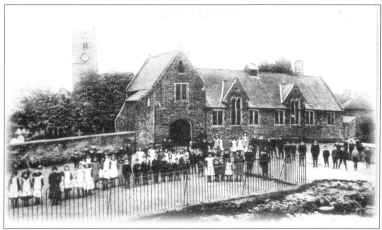

Postcard of the school stamped 10 September 1907.

Today High Bickington pupils can sit down to home-cooked lunches, which are provided by Mrs Vera Stevens. However, for a short while in 1980 this facility was withdrawn in an attempt by the Local Education Authority to save money. Meals were cooked at a central kitchen and delivered to the schools. This idea did not last long and home-cooked fare returned to the village school.

On a not-too-delicate matter, I have been told on very good authority that the toilets were the bucket type, which the caretaker emptied once a week.

Mr Archibold J. Marcom followed Mr Ham in the headship and he held an Open Day in 1927 when parents were invited to view their children's work – not an unusual phenomenon by today's standards, but quite an innovation in those days. He also requested that the boys wear uniform caps to school.

R.W. Pitman was the headmaster between 1929 and 1937 and a man who integrated with the village people in their work and play. He continued Mr Marcom's good work with the school football and netball teams and organised the first inter-school sports, with four schools competing – High Bickington, Burrington, Atherington and Umberleigh. Burrington won the silver cup that Mr Pitman had provided. He also became one of the first committee members of High Bickington Athletic Club in 1937. Although he was no longer at the school he still played an active role in the Club for many years.

Mr Pitman also wrote a history of High Bickington, which has served to provide valuable information for this book. He said that to write the book was a labour of love and dedicated it:

... to the inhabitants of High Bickington, in grateful recognition of the innumerable kindness and great good fellowship, and as a token of regard for their forebears who made the village what it is, but have no visible memorial.

In a few short years our village and its inhabitants had clearly found a place in his heart.

In 1939 the school had an influx of 88 evacuee children and four teachers from Sydenham in south-east London. The school was not large enough to accommodate them so the Church Hall became a makeshift classroom. The year 1944 saw the introduction of the eleven-plus examination and children over that age continued their education at either Chulmleigh Secondary School or Barnstaple Grammar School. When the neighbouring school at Atherington closed in 1949 the children were transferred to High Bickington. Although this move had its opponents the children soon settled in.

If the schoolmaster from 1857 visited Mrs Jackie Rudman, today's headteacher, he would find little outward change in the school. However, one glance inside would leave him astonished. To begin with the children are fit, healthy and bouncing with energy – quite a change from the undernourished, ill-dressed and sickly children of his era. Secondly, the teaching methods and equipment have improved beyond all comprehension in those intervening 143 years. Of course the three R's are always important, along with computers and IT skills, but so are art and games. In 2000 the cricket team won the North Devon Area Kwik Cricket Final and the school saw successes in football, tag-rugby and golf!

Today there are 71 pupils with three full-time teachers, two classroom assistants and an active Parent Teacher Association. These raise money for all the 'extras' that the school budget does not cover, such as computer equipment, new hymnbooks, school outings and sports equipment.

On a return visit to the school I feel that the first schoolmaster would be both shocked and delighted at today's school life. He would also no doubt be proud of the part he played in the history of the school.

～A JOURNEY ～ DOWN THROUGH THE YEARS AT HIGH BICKINGTON SCHOOL 1918–2000

Left: *Bernard Hookway (pictured c.1918) lived at Ebberley Barton and rode his pony to school. During the day he left the pony in the stables belonging to his grandfather, Bernard Cole.*

1. Bessie Newbery, 2. Mary Pidler,
3. Dorothy Goss, 4. Elsie Squire, 5. Maud Dunn, 6. Florence Parker, 7. Dulcie Slee,
8. Mr Ham, 9. Walter Huxtable. 10. Dudley Squire, 11. Annie Davis, 12. Eva Squire, 13. ?,
14. Elsie Farley, 15. Elizabeth Short, 16. Dorris Squire,
17. Florence Kent, 18. Percy Baker, 19. ? Turner, 20. Gertie Pidler,
21. Bethra Squire, 22. Audrey Snell, 23. Doris Gooding, 24. Kathleen Snell, 25. Mabel Pidler,
26. William Huxtable, 27. Dion Snell, 28. Norman Bedford, 29. Jack Pickard, 30. Harold Baker,
31. Wilfred Sanders, 32. Sidney Petherick, 33. Robert Ellicott, 34. Bill Eastman, 35. Cyril Brownscombe,
36. Bill Norman, 37. Cecil Squire, 38. Reginald Barment Slee, 39. Clifford Thomas Gooding. Photo, c.1920.

1. Clifford Thomas Gooding, 2. Cyril Brownscombe, 3. Walter Huxtable, 4. William Huxtable, 5. Dion Snell, 6. Walter Ham (Headteacher), 7. Hilda Huxtable, 8. Sidney Petherick, 9. George Thompson, 10. Bernard Hookway, 11. Frank Heales, 12. Cecil Squire, 13. Elsie Farley, 14. Letitia Tucker (teacher), 15. Elizabeth (Lizzie) Gooding, 16. Florence May Kent, 17. Doris Squire, 18. Annie Davis, 19. Mary Pidler, 20. Dulcie Slee, 21. Dorothy Goss, 22. ? Davis, younger sister of Annie, 23. Eva Squire, 24.?, 25. Reginald Slee. Photo, c.1922.

High Bickington school pupils saluting the flag at Kingford Hill House on Empire Day, c.1924.

School outing to Kingford Hill House (1925), the home of Mrs Douglas-Hamilton.
Mr Ham is seated on the left with his hat on his knee. Mrs Douglas-Hamilton is standing behind
Mr Ham. Teachers Miss Tucker and Miss Newbery are 4th and 5th from the right.

High Bickington School, c.1928. Left to right, back: Miss Newbery, Percy Guard, Donald Wythe,
Edgar Cole, John Tucker, Harold Turner, Willoughby Eastman, Kitchener Kent, Harold Eastman,
Tommy Davy; middle: Nora Norman, Mary Clatworthy, Evelyn Sussex, Dorothy Snell,
Mary Marshall, Phyllis Eastman, Irene King, Irene Guard, Mary Eastman;
front: Steve Tucker, Jim Parker, Stan Tucker.

High Bickington School, 1930. School teacher Letitia (Tish) Tucker with her class.
Left to right, back row: Stanley Gooding, Cecil Clatworthy, Dick Tapscott, ? Eastman, Dougie Bale,
Reg Parker, Jim Turner; middle: Joan Davis, Rosie Smith, May Cole, Evelyn Smith, Phyllis James,
Queenie Merryfield; front: John Guard, Millicent Baker, Reggie Johns.

High Bickington School, 1938. Left to right, back row: Rosalie Smith, John Pidler, Jack Down,
Wallace Turner, Betty Tapscott; middle: Mary Wonnacott, Iris Ellicott, Doreen Heale, Avis Baker,
Dorothy Woollacott, Joyce Huxtable, Audrey Baker, Lorna Snell;
seated: Bill Smith, Eric Bolt, Eric Parker, Dick Pidler, Ronald Turner, Ronald Huxtable.

The teacher on the left is Miss Vickery and the teacher on the right Miss Harris.
Left to right, back row: Brian Hewlett, Norman White, John Huxtable, Michael Squire, Michael
Trigger, George Parker, Graham Copp, Richard Tucker, John Harris; 3rd row: Daphne Gammon,
Jacqueline Shapland, Christine Squire, Sylvia Brown, Janet Wythe, ? Milton, Clare Plummer;
2nd row: ?, Marion Goss, ? Luxton, Pat Goss, Barbara Gill, Josephine Armstrong, Josephine Trigger,
Pat Perkins, Christopher Hare; sitting: Dennis Huxtable, Philip Keen, Timothy Shapland, Barry
Tapscott, Roger Hockridge, Jimmy Tucker, Michael Tucker, Ernest Luxton. Photograph, 1954.

The class of 1965 perched on their games climbing frame in the school playground.

Sports Day, 1969/70. 1. Alan Tapscott, 2. Peter Glover, 3. Gary Mitchell, 4. Carolyn Milton, 5. Angela Butt, 6. Lorna St John, 7. Ashley Underhill, 8. Steve Down, 9. Kevin Short, 10. Graham Down, 11. Keith St John, 12. Christopher Jay, 13. Linda St John.

Left to right, back row: Robert Ashley, John Laramy, Darren Baker, Jonathan Smith, Tracey Petherick, Paul Jones, Perry Barrow, Philip Thomas, Andrew Webber, ?, David Webber; 3rd row: Nicholas Copp, David Neil, Trudy Short, Barry Clemens, Timothy House, Simon Beer, ?, Stephen Glover, Stephen Johnson, Jeremy Beer, Gillian Weeks; 2nd row: Jane Adams, Claire Tucker, Tracey Cullen, Jonathan Rowden, Richard Tapscott, Sam Pearce, John Drayton, Stephen Herniman, Craig Petherick, Steve Webber, Mr Lloyd; front: ?, Claire Thomas, Judith Ashley, Gillian Herniman, Lee Tucker, Jonathon Tapscott, Simn Copp, Giles Rowden. Photograph, 1980/81.

The group photograph of the school had to be taken indoors that year - 1985.

The group photograph was taken in 1989 in the shade of the trees in the churchyard.
Left to right, back row: head teacher Mrs Abbott, Bobby Maud, Cary Ann Gillett, David Fish,
Andrew Thomas, ?, Ross Cornish, Stephen Clemens, Anthony Wallis, Mark Milton, Kaye Seaward,
Nancy Rose, Mrs Cox; 3rd row: Louise Clarke, Maria Barratt, Ben Dennis, Sarah Westward,
Michelle ?, Philippa Kingdom, Amy Cannon, Amy Drayton, Philip Smith, Richard Maud,
Samantha Roulestone, Ross Cannon, Daniel Wearne; 2nd row: Jamie Carne, Debra Hedges,
Jason Tapscott, Joe Kingdom, Alistair McCoy, Nicholas Brown, John Milton, Paul Kingdom,
Julian Beer, Rebecca Heal, Billy King, Kate Robinson; front: David Pugsley, Simon Woollacott,
Christopher Beer, Lucy Hedges, Kelly-Marie Brown, Fiona Stewart, Heather Dawson, ?, Ian ?,
Philip Cross, Peter Robertson, Christopher ?.

Left and above: *A young St Trinian's schoolgirl entering for the fancy dress at the school fête, 1999. Left to right: Verity Lunn, June Webber and granddaughter Megan Sanders. Meanwhile mums serve the teas and hot dogs from the window of the school kitchen.* (Both A.S.)

High Bickington School, 2000. Left to right, back row: Sadie Foster, Brian Stevens, Lauren Michael, Thomas Sanders, Rachel Wingate, Rosie Hedges, Nathan Gray, Eddie Hedges, Melanie Pert, Kim Short, Samantha Short, Erica Beer, Louise Peck, Thomas Phillips, Mark Lambourne;
4th row: Mrs Seaward (Secretary) Mrs Strickland (Classroom Assistant), Jason Jones, Katherine Reeves, Joe Raymont, Jessica Brook, Sinead Delahaye, Verity Lunn, Megan Sanders, Lauren Reeves, Casey Delahaye, Louise Lambourne, Patrick Tucker, Joshua Phillips, Katie Tucker, Katrina Miller, Mrs Stevens (Kitchen Manager), Mrs Hutchings (Classroon Assistant);
3rd row: Jodie Sanders, James Brown, George Strachen, Alice Alford, Mathew Cummings, Peter Short, Ivana Gray, Simeon Gray, Daniel Lambourne, Sam Raymont, Beth Avery, Amy Keitch, Ryan Brooks, John Paul Cowley-Young, David Down;
2nd row: Ben Povey, Elizabeth Johnson, Christopher Maris, Danny Povey, Christian Beagly, Emma Underhill, Mr Rob Norton (Class 1 teacher), Mrs Keren Beazley (Class 2 teacher), Mrs Jackie Rudman (Headteacher), Caroline Harquard (Reception teacher), Kelly Marie Cowley-Young, Peter Gray, Scott Pert, Mathew Walker, Grace Alford, Alexander Phillips.
sitting: Leslie Milton, Indiana Beer, Joshua Crook, Nicole Short, Francesca De Sequeira, Amber Buckpilt, Ben Isaac, Frazer Reeves, Georgina Phillips, Peter Underhill, Chloe Jones.

The church before 1945 showing the diamond-shaped clock face. The original tower was the tall part of the building next to the porch.

The church after 1945 – the clock face is round and note that the gravestones are all neatly lined up in rows.

Chapter 11
Religious Affairs

High Bickington has one church and two chapels, all within the precincts of the village. I will start with the oldest, the parish Church of St Mary which has stood in one form or another at the centre of the village for more than 1000 years.

King Athelstan was the grandson of King Alfred the Great and reigned between AD924–939. During his lifetime he resided in different parts of his kingdom which stretched from southern Scotland to the borders of Wales and Cornwall. In AD930 whilst staying at a riverside 'palace' in Umberleigh, he founded the first church at High Bickington.

In 1620 the antiquary Tristram Risdon wrote that the king endowed the parishes of Atherington and High Bickington 'with two hides of land that remain in the possession of the pastor today'. The resident priest was also given permission to:

... cut wood to build a house from the kings holt [woodland] and to graze his beasts therein. Fuel for his hearth and pannage [food] for his sows and pig. World without end.

This first church would have been constructed of wood and cob with a thatched roof. After 1066 when the village had become a Norman manor and the Church of England had undergone some reorganisation, another church, this time made of stone although still thatched, was built on the site where St Mary's stands today. The font dates back to these times, as does some of the stonework on the south side of the chancel. The font was made from only two pieces of stone but the story goes that once when it was being cleaned it collapsed into 45 pieces. It was a painstaking job to put this jigsaw together. Local craftsman Arthur Down made the wooden cover.

Around 1450 the church was enlarged and was at this point very much as it stands today. The north

View of St Mary's towards the alter, 1998. Note the barrel wagon ceiling.
(A.S.)

aisle was added and the west tower erected. The present vestry is all that is left of the Norman tower. Remains of an old stairway can be seen in the vestry wall. The rector at this time was a John Compton, who died in 1453 and is buried in the chancel. It is thought he was responsible for the improvements to the church.

The 19th century found the interior of the church being restored again. Pews were re-sited and the screen and minstrels' gallery between the nave and chancel were removed. Parts of the gallery were used to repair other structures such as the pew-ends. The north door was blocked and the church walls and ceiling were plastered. However, the wagon roof-beams with medieval carved bosses were left exposed. I always find the ceiling of St Mary's photographically dramatic.

The organ – which had replaced a string band – was moved from the vestry to its present position. It is still going well although it needs £15 000 spent on it to keep it in good working order. The pulpit was dedicated in 1839 and replaced in 1942 by another rescued from a blitzed church in Exeter. This was installed in memory of the Revd Cecil Wansbrough MA, High Bickington's rector for 45 years.

THE PEW-ENDS

Any visitor to St Mary's will note that some of its finest features are the 70 magnificently carved pew-ends. There is no written evidence of where these ends came from. Before the reign of the Tudors it was normal for the congregation to stand or kneel for the duration of the service. After the enlargement of the church in the 15th century it is likely the pews were then installed.

Following the destruction of churches and monasteries during Henry VIII's reign (1509–47) it is

Revd Wansbrough and Dean Gamble of Exeter Cathedral outside the school, 1928.

An unidentified photo found in the church album, probably of a church or parish committee.
Left to right, back: Bill Newbery, ?, ?, Revd Wansbrough; 3rd row: George Pidler, John Cole, ?, ?, ?,
Walter Ham (teacher); 2nd row: ?, Eli Harris, ?, Elon Cole, Bernard Cole; front: ?, Joe Tucker.

Linda Rowden, Greta Squire and May Miller with just a few of the kneelers made by the ladies of St Mary's Guild. (A.S.)

Bellringers at St Mary's Flower Festival, 1999. Far left at the back is Stephen Herniman; left to right, front row: Roger Keen, John Down, Margaret ?, Edgar Cole, Christine Ley, Cecil Crocker. (A.S.)

Above: *Repairing the wooden flooring under the pews in the west end of St Mary's, 2000. Note that there are no foundations, only earth.* (A.S.)

Left: *Pew-end, 2000.*

possible that the pews were reclaimed and brought to St Mary's. The earliest are thought to be 12th or 13th century. The pew-ends have several different styles. There are carvings of flowers, foliage, corn, wheat and animals.

The bases of many pews show signs of wear, either from woodworm or damp. There is no way of telling if this was as a result of them standing on the earthen floor at High Bickington or elsewhere. Recently, when pews were removed from the back of the church (because the timbers beneath were rotted), I was amazed to see that there was no solid foundation, only earth.

Mrs Siddie Greenwood-Penny, who lived at Nethergrove, carved the choirstall frontalls. Her son Dr Robert Augustus Greenwood-Penny drew the design of a procession of animals. On one stall the inscription reads 'O all ye fowls of the air bless ye

the Lord' and, on the other side, 'O all ye beasts and cattle, bless ye the Lord. Praise him and magnify him for ever' – this is taken from the canticle 'Benedicite Omnia Opera'. Siddie died in 1903 before the carvings were completed and Dr Arnold Good and his brother Thomas finished them.

Most of the carvings in the rest of the church are of people, all with their own story to tell. For those interested in this intriguing subject I suggest that you read *The Pew Ends of High Bickington Church* and the Brief History and *Guide Book of St Mary's, High Bickington*, both by E.J. Winter.

I must mention the 'green men' of St Mary's. An authority on the subject has told me that it has more carvings of them than any other church. The green man is a pagan symbol and at the time when the church was being built or furnished the workmen were not all Christian, so, to 'hedge their bets', they hid some of their own symbols among the Christian carvings.

THE KNEELERS

When admiring the carved pews it is impossible to forget the excellent needlecraft of the kneelers. They depict the theme of the countryside and have been made by the members of St Mary's Guild. Each kneeler has a St Mary's rose emblem worked into a corner.

In 1980 Guild members Linda Rowden, Greta Squire, Mary Buck and Nora Cole travelled to Kennerleigh, near Crediton, for tapestry lessons. They came back and passed on their newly-acquired skills to the rest of the group. The results bring many a compliment from visitors to the church.

THE CLOCK

The clock is a two-train, wrought-iron frame, 'birdcage' turret clock designed to show the time on a single external dial and strike the hour on the tenor bell. The clock mechanism was originally hand wound but now has two automatic winding units. The clock has no maker's name on it but is thought to have been made by John Cole of Barnstaple, who died in 1757. From the churchwarden's accounts we see that John Cole and his brother were paid to repair the clock in 1742. Other clocks made by him in 1734 for Combe Martin, Northam and Ilfracombe have been replaced – therefore our clock could have historic significance, especially since the overhaul in 1999 by David Jones of The Lizard, Cornwall, has meant that the clock now keeps good time.

In 1947 the original diamond-shaped, blue wooden face was replaced by a convex copper dial. It had been recovered from the ruins of a church destroyed in the blitz in London and was given as a memorial to the men of the village who died in the war. This was also restored in 1999. All the costs of projects such as clock repairs, the installation of heating and lighting, and also the repairs to the church tower in the year 2000, are funded by St Mary's Guild, a group of ladies who raise money by flower festivals, jumble sales, sales of work, fêtes and similar events.

Top: *David Jones renovating the clock face, 1999.*

Centre: *One of the builders emerging from the small doorway on the roof of the tower.* (Both A.S.)

Below: *Sally Webb, May Miller and Eileen Thorne of St Mary's Guild arranging a sale of work, 2000.* (A.S.)

*The six old bells that had been refurbished and the two new ones that according to Bernard Cole's
diary were rung for the first time on 4 March 1911.
The 5th from the left is Revd Wansbrough, 6th from the left is Dr Good
and on the end is John Down.*

*Bellringing competition at High Bickington, 1947.
In the group can be seen Revd Plummer, Bill Pidler, Jack Kent, Ernest Quick, Jack Heddon,
Jack Down, Bob Pidler, Dick Pidler, Cecil Clatworthy, Lewis Brownscombe.*

Another competition at St Mary's, 1930. The following are known: 28: Louie Brownscombe, 30: William Newbery, 31: Charlie Squire, 53: Ernest Quick, 61: Robert Gill Pidler, 62: Revd Wansbrough, 64: George Pidler with sheild, 69: Jack Down, 71: Jack Headon, 72: Leonard Woollacott, 75: Leslie Brownscombe, 76: Bill Pidler, 77: Herbert Pidler, 78: John Kent, 80: George Morrish, 81: Frank Heales.

A bellringers' outing at East Cocker, 1962. Included are: A. Short, ?, E. Cole, A. Snell, C. Gooding, J. Patt, D. Pidler, A. Down, C. Shapland, R. Slee, B. Hookway, S. Down, C. Bright, A. Tapscott,' W. Pidler, H. Pidler, ?, G. Tucker. The four men at the back are: G. Keen, K. Snell, J. Down, C. Miller.

The two new bells, 1911. Dr Good is on the left and Ernest Pidler is on the right.

THE BELLS

The original five bells were cast in 1753 and in 1827 the sixth one was added. At a Vestry meeting in January 1911, it was decided to restore and rehang the six bells and add two more to complete the octave, the larger bell of the two to be the tenor and the smaller to be a treble. Four of the other bells were to be recast half a tone flatter. The work cost £351.11s.1d. and the sum was raised within 15 months.

St Mary's bellringers have a long and successful history of winning competitions down through the years. In 1938 Robert Gill Pidler, a churchwarden, was made captain of the bellringers, and in 1955 his son Herbert took on the mantle and kept the post until 1986. Gerald Herniman succeeded him and is still the captain today. With the help of his wife Wendy and Roger Keen they are trying to revive interest in this ancient art and are always looking out for people interested in joining their team of bellringers.

THE PAROCHIAL CHURCH COUNCIL

For the purpose of this book I was lent the PCC minute book which started in 1883. It took me several days to read through and make notes of the events that took place over these past 117 years. It was exciting to read about the parish people that I had been researching. The names in *Kelly's Directory* and on the 1891 census came alive; I felt that I was a silent member at their meetings.

On 26 March, 1883, a Vestry meeting was held at 11 o'clock in the forenoon for the purpose of appointing overseers and any other business. The following list of ratepayers was proposed as the list of overseers for the parish:

MR JOHN COLE MR JOHN TURNER
MR JOSEPH COLE MR SAMUEL DUNN
MR SIMON GOSS MR THOMAS DOWN

It was proposed by Mr Harris of Lee and seconded by Mr Arthur Squire that Mr Eli Harris and Mr Thomas Down be appointed assessors. The rector was Richard Yerburgh. These appointments were all related to the distribution of the Poor Laws.

I believe these first meetings were held in the church because in May 1887 the notice reads that the Vestry meeting was to be held in the schoolroom.

These gatherings were held to appoint officers of the church, such as wardens and those on councils and committees. Reports were also made on church accounts, the conditions of the building and church-yard. They were also an opportunity for the vicar to thank his officers for the previous year's work.

On 5 July 1883 a meeting was called for ratepayers and farmers to discuss supplying the village with 'pure water'. The idea was rejected as it was thought the village was sufficiently supplied. (Perhaps there would not have been a water supply problem in the first part of the 20th century if the 1883 decision had been more positive.).

At the Easter Vestry meeting of 1884 I found the first mention of churchwardens. The Revd Yerburgh appointed Robert Gill as his churchwarden and Arthur Squire was made parish churchwarden. Later this post was called the people's churchwarden.

After the Education Department reported that the infant's classroom was too small a meeting on 13 March 1891 agreed to put 2d. in the £1 on the Rates to aid a fund to enlarge the school building.

By 1893 many now familiar names were appearing at the yearly meeting:

MR THOMAS DUNFORD, HEALE TOWN
MR HENRY SQUIRE, HOOPERS
MR STEPHEN HELLYER, LITTLE BICKINGTON
MRS MARY COLE, CULVERHOUSE (THE FIRST WOMAN)
MR ROBERT GREENWOOD-PENNY, NETHERGROVE
MR JAMES WOOLLACOTT, YELLAND
MR ELI HARRIS AND WILLIAM MANNING
(APPOINTED AS ASSESSORS)
MR THOMAS BOUNDY (APPOINTED AS WAYWARDEN)

Mr Thomas Boundy (appointed as waywarden)
Mr James Harris
(appointed Guardian of the Parish).
Others present were:
Mr R. Pidler   Mr Goss
Mr Pincombe   Mr Peake
Mr Slee (Libbaton)
Mr Down (Southwood)
Mr Eastmond (Shutely)

Revd Wansbrough's first meeting was on 11 April 1897 when he remarked on the sad loss sustained by the parish through the death of General Gardiner who had been the rector's churchwarden since 1886.

The year 1903 saw the offer from Mrs Gardiner of a stained-glass window for the chancel in memory of her husband and three years later in 1907 £7.5s.0d. was spent on repairing the working of the clock and painting the face. April 1923 saw the retirement of Eli Harris of Weirmarsh and Dr Good became the People's Warden.

Although Mrs Wansbrough paid for the Church Hall to be built in 1925, the first mention of it was at a meeting in 1926 when it was agreed to allow the Methodist chapel to use the piano for a service in the building. In 1929, along with Revd Wansbrough, Dr Good, Mr Newbery, Mr Kent, Mr Davis and Mr W. Pidler, there were 12 ladies at the meeting - petticoat power had come to High Bickington! At this meeting it was also voted to replace the churchyard path and pay the two organ blowers a salary of £1.2s 6d. a year.

March 1932 saw the death of Dr Good, and Mrs Good was at the meeting (as she was for many more years). Also at this meeting it was apparent how popular the outings had become for the Sunday School, the choir and the bellringers. In April 1934 the Revd Jones was appointed as Curate. In 1938 Revd Wansbrough retired. Mr R.G. Pidler was made churchwarden and captain of bellringers, and tribute was paid to the late Mr William Newbery. Dr and Mrs Graham-Pole joined the PCC.

In 1939 new bell ropes were purchased and a new design drawn up for wooden doors in the school porch. The following year, 1940, Colonel Maxwell offered his resignation as churchwarden due to the unavoidable circumstances of war and the restrictions on car use. The council persuaded him to stay.

In 1945 Revd Jones left and Revd Plummer arrived. In 1947 Mrs Wansbrough died aged eighty. In 1950 it was remarked that there had been no deaths in the parish that year. Mrs Martin Thompson (a deaconess) asked to assist in services - perhaps this lady made another first for the rights of women in the church?

In 1951 we see the first mention of a church magazine, which was distributed by Mrs Pickard. Miss Newbery and Miss Tucker ran the Sunday School and Mrs Thompson was still assisting at services. The following year was a successful one for the bellringing festival, a scout troop was started by Police Constable Swift and the £100 bequeathed by Mrs Wansbrough was spent on repairing the organ.

In 1955 came the death of Mr R.G. Pidler, churchwarden and captain of bellringers. On a lighter note, 1959 saw the report of woodworm in the organ! Reports that the Church Hall was badly in need of repair came in 1962.

In 1970 Revd Plummer's 25 years in the parish were celebrated with a Flower Festival and a united service with the Methodist Church and North Road Chapel - 1974 was Revd Plummer's last year. Revd Bines arrived in 1975 and left four years later to be replaced by Revd Barratt.

St Mary's Guild began in 1981 (at least there is no mention of it before) and the *Rectory Ramblings* started with 146 copies being sold - in the year 2000, the magazine is still going strong with 250 copies being sold each month and it is now a community project without any direct links with the church.

Revd Gillett arrived in 1985 and in 1986 he wrote that close co-operation between North Road Chapel and the Methodist Church continued with their monthly united services. The Church Hall was back in service with improved appearance and facilities. The Flower Festival, which lasted four days, was an increasing success. Herbert Pidler retired as captain of the bellringers and Gerald Herniman took over.

In 1994 Revd Gillett retired and Hugh Pollock eventually arrived, followed in 1999 by the Revd John Carvosso, the first rector of High Bickington not to live in the village. He has the responsibility for Tawstock, Atherington and High Bickington and therefore has no reason to leave his original house in Tawstock.

Let me end this account with an incident that happened to Mr Dick Farley in the 1930s when he was sexton and grave digger. One day some local lads had once again climbed up the trees along the avenue in the churchyard. Dick Farley, who took great pride in his job, was determined to catch them. He told them in no uncertain terms that he would wait there until they came down and then 'Cleave down the little blighters!'. He made himself comfortable under one of the trees to await their descent - then promptly fell asleep! When he awoke it had grown dark and the lads had soft-footed it away.

Clockwise from top:
*Revd Septimus Palmer
MA (1850-69);
Revd Cecil Vaughen
Wansbrough MA
(1897-1937);
Revd Arthur Jasper
Plummer MA
(1945-74);
Revd Christopher
Barratt (1979-83);
Revd Vincent Gillett
MSc, F Coll, P
(1984-94);
Revd Hugh Pollock
meets Mr John Tucker
after morning
service, 1999;
Revd John Carvosso
(1999-time of writing).*

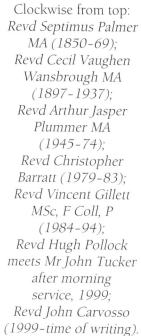

Presentation to Revd Wansbrough on his retirement, 1937.
Left to right, standing: Bill Newbery, Robert Pidler, Revd Wansbrough, Mrs Barton,
Col Maxwell; seated Revd Jones and Mrs Wansbrough. (R.L.K.)

Above: *Revd Gillett scooting around his parish, 1985.*

Right: *A windy day planting winter bulbs, 2000. Left to right: Mrs Ruth Carvosso, Revd John Carvosso, Mrs Jane Gibson.* (A.S.)

Above right: *Outside St Mary's, 1994. Left to right: Desmond Clapton (churchwarden), Mr Roger Keen (CC), Mrs Gillett, Mrs Betty Harpum (churchwarden), Mr John Tucker (CC), Revd Gillett, Archdecon's wife, Archdeacon of Barnstaple, William Lewis (the organist from Rose Ash).*

Above: *The wedding of Ern Pidler and Beattie Way. The bridesmaid on the right was Mrs Evelyn Down (née Hellyer).*

Top right: *Sydney and Greta Squire on their wedding day, 24 April 1937.*

Above right: *The wedding of Ken Gill and Dorothy Snell, 1940. On the left is Mrs Nancy Gill and on the right Mary Ann and Lewis Snell.* (R.L.K.)

Right: *Mary Gertrude Evelyn Crossing marries Dr Arnold Saxty Good at Berkley, Frome, 1913.*

Far right: *The wedding of Sarah Tucker and John Reeve, 1985.*

Bottom right: *Doris (née Gooding) and Herbert Pidler of Dadlands arrive for their wedding reception at the Church Hall.*

Above: *George Harris of Presbrey married Eleanor Harris of Weirmarsh, 1908. Eleanor's father Eli Harris is seated on the right.*

Right: *The Parker family at the wedding of Ned Parker and Mary (née Eastman), c.1900.*

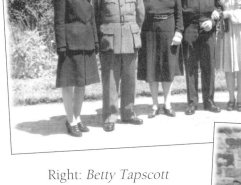

Left: *Wartime bride Mary Cooke of 1, South View, married Keith Dodd in 1940. He was in the Australian Air Force and stationed at RAF Chivenor. During the war he was shot down over the Mediterranean. He swam ashore but was captured and spent time as a prisoner-of-war. After the war the couple returned to Australia. Mary keeps in regular contact with her village friends.*

Right: *Betty Tapscott and Fred Netherway get married at St Mary's Church, 1948.*

The Zion Chapel built in 1834 by the Bible Christians, now the Methodist chapel.

Interior of the building - this photograph is at least 100 years old.

THE METHODIST CHAPEL

The Zion Chapel, built in 1834, stands where Back Lane meets Pows Lane. The Bible Christians first registered it as a place of worship on 25 July 1834 but it is known to have been in use before that. For information on the chapel, I have relied heavily on research complied by Margaret Bolt.

The piece of land the chapel stands on was purchased for £10.10s.0d. from Robert Marshall, a shopkeeper from Chulmleigh. The 1840 tithe map of High Bickington shows that Robert Marshall owned 25 acres of land in the area where the chapel was built. The trustees at the time were James Brooks who was a Minister of the Gospel, John Allin, a Yeoman of High Bickington, Thomas Squance, a miller of Tawstock, Joseph Tremeer, a tea dealer of South Molton, William Babbage, yeoman of Burrington, and William Buckingham, a shoe-maker from Filleigh.

It is almost certain the members of the chapel would have had to carry out the building work at their own expense. When it was first built it had a gallery across the back of the hall. To reach it there were stairs from inside the main door. This gallery was later removed. A stable housing the preacher's

horse and another out building were demolished in 1893 when the schoolroom was built on to the chapel. In April 1861 a magazine tells us that 'a tea meeting was held to promote the secular education of the young, apart from State Education or ecclesiastical intolerance', in the village on 7 January 1861. An excellent tea was given to the children and a public tea followed to which 73 persons sat down – far more than expected in view of the extreme severity of the weather. A meeting followed addresses by Brothers W. Manning and E. Gudridge, on the advantages of education. The purpose of the meeting was to assist in the providing salary of the person engaged to instruct the children. It was noted that:

He is a pious young man, a member of the Society and suited to the work in which he is engaged. Proceeds of the tea £2.12s.6d. The school has been founded about 18 months. It has since its commencement increased in number and influence and, we hope, been a benefit to the neighbourhood.

There was also a Sunday School where in 1904 there were 28 scholars with seven teachers, six of whom were listed as teetotal, as were 22 of the scholars!

The High Bickington Methodist Sunday-School outing, c.1920. This photograph was taken at Bishops Tawton where they had tea. Left to right, standing at the back: Edwin Down, Wilfred Dunn, Mary Eastman, Percy Bolt, Reginald Wonnacott, William Gooding; back, sitting: Tom Goss, Walter Petherbridge, Bill Eastman, Fred Eastman, John Baker, Percy Baker; middle: Harold Baker, Dulcie Slee, Frankie Walker, Doris Gooding, Reginald Slee, Joyce Slee, Bill Goss, Marjorie Goss; front: Sidney Petherbridge, Harold, Annie and Maud Eastman, Gwen Down, Tom Wonnacott, Agnes Down, Vera Wonnacott. Note the hobnailed boots even with their Sunday best!

Far right: *The chapel in North Road.*

Above: *The Kingfisher Club, 1969, organised by Jonathan, Mark and Nina Thomas at the chapel. In the group are: Heather Bolt, Susan Pidler, Stuart Mitchell, Michael Bright, Alan Pidner, Heather Lawson, Peter Tucker, David Martin, Ashley Underhill, Nigel Clathworthy, Kathleen Bolt and Sarah Tucker.*

Right: *Christingle Service at St Mary's Church, High Bickington, 1999.* (A.S.)

Below: *Palm Sunday procession with a donkey, 1993, a United Churches service held at St Mary's.* (R.L.)

Above: *Sylvia Pidler in 1999 at the Zion Chapel organ where she has played for 55 years.* (A.S.)

THE BIBLE CHRISTIANS

The Bible Christians, a small nonconformist denomination, started at Lake Farm, Shebbear, in 1815, and quickly spread throughout North Devon. They held meetings in members' houses. In 1819 George Cooper of High Bickington registered his house for a Bible Christian meeting. Between 1820 and 1834 several other houses were registered for the same purpose.

In 1821 the Clergy Returns show the question: 'Have you any Papists or Dissenters?' The rector at High Bickington, William Palmer Stanwell, wrote: 'A few Methodists – no resident teacher, one inhabited house, lately licensed, open to any itinerant preachers.'

In 1831 there were services listed once every two weeks and the first child to be baptised in the Zion Chapel was Arthur Milford in 1838. By 1848 there were Sunday services at 3.00p.m. and 6.00p.m. and on Thursdays at 7.00p.m. Membership in 1862 was 28. It rose and fell during the following years until there were 55 members in 1907, which was the beginning of United Methodism.

The layout of the Zion Chapel is of typical Bible-Christian style with a raised dais for the choir and no communion rail. Bible Christians always took the elements seated, which were probably brought to them by the Elders. The pews and pulpit were added later and the Communion table was made in 1919 by an ex-Sunday-School scholar and his friend Ernest Pidler.

Music usually plays a part in religious services and High Bickington Bible Christians were no different. In the beginning there were very few musical instruments and singing was accompanied by a violin or flute. As there were few hymn books the preacher would read out a couple of lines and the congregation followed in song. By 1890 there was an organ but no organist! Mr William Gooding taught himself to play and wrote in his diary that if he made a mistake he would just sing a little louder.

In 1957, after 35 years of accompanying the singing, it was found that the organ had a bad case of woodworm. A committee was formed and it was decided to purchase a pipe organ. However, there was not enough room to install it in the chapel. This problem was solved when Mrs Snell, who lived next door in Prospect House, sold them a piece of land for one shilling to build an extension to house the organ. Unfortunately, by 1983, moth and silverfish had wrought so much damage that the organ had to be overhauled and repaired to the painful tune of £2127. 50p. Rather an expensive meal for any moth!

Today the Methodists hold services every Sunday at 11a.m. and regular monthly United services with St Mary's Church. There is a thriving Sunday School and two children's clubs. They also link up with St Mary's Church for several services during the year, including Christingle, Plough Service, Palm Sunday, Rogation, Armistice and an open-air service which is held in the summer.

NORTH ROAD CHAPEL

The chapel was built in 1834 on a piece of wasteland measuring 50ft x 30ft and named Bickington Green. It stands opposite the Golden Lion public house. The land was purchased in 1826 for the 'purpose of erecting a chapel to be used for preaching of the Gospel and the gathering a Church of Christ to be governed by the rules of the New Testament.'

In July 1913 the Ebenezer Hall was opened on the site of the old Brethren Chapel which had been in a dilapidated and unsatisfactory condition and was demolished six months before. The new one built by Darch and Son of Yarnscombe cost £300.

Another interesting discovery was made in the year 2000 when Margaret Wright from Nottingham came in search of her 'roots'. Her great-grandfather was Robert Payne, a shoemaker in High Bickington in the mid 1800s. With the help of a plan of St Mary's churchyard which Syd Squire made she found the gravestone of Robert who died in 1873 aged 57. But where was her great-grandmother Rachel? On the way back to her car Margaret looked over the wall of North Road Chapel and saw gravestones. She decided to investigate and found Rachel Payne who had died aged 44 in 1857, sixteen years before her husband. Why were husband and wife buried apart?

There was a clue to this is in a newspaper cutting of 1868 in a letter to the editor of the *North Devon Journal* headed 'Priestly Bigotry and Intolerance' on another matter – the death after a short illness of James Kelly, the 17 year-old son of the High Bickington tailor. Rector of St Mary's, Septimus Palmer, had refused to bury him in the churchyard because the young man had not been baptised. This caused much grief among the family and friends but Septimus stood by his decision although he agreed that the body could be interred in the churchyard after nightfall – the followers, however, were to go no further than the entrance.

This made the loved ones of the deceased 'even more afflicted'. However, someone had told the minister of the Brethren Chapel, Mr R. Payne of the matter, and the funeral was held the next day with a large crowd of sympathising but indignant friends.

The letter of 1868 happens to mention that burials had been discontinued at the chapel 'due to sanitary considerations', which sheds light on why Robert, who was obviously a minister of the chapel, was not buried in its graveyard with his wife when he died in 1873.

The Brethren Chapel was once known for its large revival meetings, which were held in tents in a farmer's field at the top of Shoplands Lane. The chapel also had a day school in the late 1800s. In a logbook at High Bickington School it states that as the chapel school was closing the children were being moved across to the church school.

By the late 1990s the congregation had dwindled and the chapel was closed for services. However, after a get deal of hard work, mainly carried out by David Brown, it has a new role as a community centre where there is a youth club and a Bible-study group. A coffee morning is held twice a month and there are plans for a luncheon club for the elderly – which only goes to show that there is plenty of life left in this old building yet.

Above: *Members of the Youth Club painting a mural on the wall at the Meeting Point which was the old Brethren Chapel in North Road, 2000.*

Top right: *Gordon Thomas painting the windows of the chapel preparing for its new use as the Meeting Point, 2000.* (A.S.)

Right: *David Brown renovating and restoring the building.*

Below right: *Maurice Ridd digging below the foundations at the start of the renovations.*

Chapter 12
The Gentry

In the hierarchy of the class system 100 years ago the largest land-owner or the lord of the manor would have been at the top of the social tree. In High Bickington the largest land-owners were the Pyncombe Estate trustees. They were, of course, an unknown faceless group of people who had little or no contact with the parishioners. Their place was therefore taken by the wealthy who owned the largest and most impressive houses.

The doctor and the rector held a unique position inasmuch as they were accepted easily by both the gentry and the common man. They would convey the problems of the poor to the affluent. The working man was too humble to share his problems with his 'betters' and when in contact with them the most he would do would be to touch his forelock.

There was no such thing as Social Security or the National Health Service and the gentry felt duty bound to care for the less well off in their parish. Between them they were responsible for the health and the moral, spiritual, recreational and, in High Bickington's case, artistic educational welfare of the people.

The largest land-owner after the Pyncombe Estate was Robert Greenwood-Penny who lived at Nethergrove. After he died, Nethergrove was sold at auction along with his properties of Middlewood, Northwood and Southwood Farms and Wards Cottage. Robert Greenwood-Penny and his wife Sarah (always known as Siddie) came with their family to High Bickington in 1883. Robert was a clever and gifted man interested in science, photography and machinery and also in architecture and natural history. He took great care of his estate and those who worked on it. Robert was the Revd Wansbrough's churchwarden from 1897 until his death in 1905, a school governor for many years and a member of the Taw and Torridge Board of Conservators. A keen sportsman who loved shooting and fishing, he was a familiar figure on the banks of the Taw during the salmon season.

Above: Siddie Greenwood-Penny, c.1890.
Below: Left to right: Revd Wansbrough, Dr Good, Robert Greenwood-Penny (small boy), Sidney's eldest son, Mrs Wansbrough, Gus Greenwood-Penny and Mrs Sidney Greenwood-Penny, 1908.

Nethergrove, c.1900, the home of the Greenwood-Pennys.

*The first car to arrive in High Bickington. Medical students Sidney and Augustus
Greenwood-Penny drove down to Nethergrove from London to visit their parents.*
(By kind permission of the Beaford Archive)

Colonel Channer on the left and Edwin Ellicott in a Rally car with the horses in tandem, c.1904.

Employees of Colonel and Mrs Channer of The Sycamores, c.1900.
Left to right: Jack Kent (gardener), ?, Edwin Ellicott (chauffeur),
?, ?, ?, ? Preston (gamekeeper).

Left: *Nethergrove, c.1930, from a post-card. (R.L.K.)*

Below: *Wards Cottage, c.1930, with Nethergrove in the background*

Siddie was a keen horsewoman and she also loved cycling. She was interested in art and was a gifted wood carver. The fronts of the choir stalls in St Mary's Church are her handiwork. Sadly she died in 1903 before they were completed.

Robert and Siddie Greenwood-Penny had four children. Robert Augustus, the eldest, was 12 when the family moved to Nethergrove and like his father he loved the country life. He became a psychiatrist and was superintendent of the female wing of the Devon County Mental Hospital at Exminster. He was a cousin and close friend of Dr Arnold Saxty Good, and the two spent many hours enjoying their shared interests in country pursuits in and around High Bickington.

Nethergrove carries the unhealed scars of a severe fire many years ago. It is, however, still a magnificent building standing serenely on the hillside overlooking the Taw valley.

After a career in the Indian Army spanning 40 years, General Percy Fortescue Gardiner, his wife Ann and his two sisters moved to the village in 1881. They lived at The Sycamores, a large Georgian house on the main road on the edge of the village. The General lived the life of a wealthy country gentleman and had a large staff, both indoors and outside. He did his duty as churchwarden for many years. He died in 1896 at the age of 75 and his wife moved to Bishops Teignton where she survived him by 50 years. She kept in close contact with many friends they had made in the village.

Next at The Sycamores was another Indian Army family, that of Colonel Bernard Channer DSO and his wife, who lived there until the Colonel died in 1905. Nora Maynard remembers that when she was a child she loved to visit Mrs Channer who she described as a dumpy lady with lots of rings on her fingers. She also recalls that Mrs Channer made her own chocolates.

Iris Wickett (née Ellicott) told of her grandfather Edwin who was the Channer's chauffeur, and she believes they owned the first car in the village. Edwin met his wife, Elizabeth Jane, when she came to live with her aunt, Mrs Morrish, who lived in Nethergrove Lodge House. Elizabeth Jane later became a lady's maid to the Misses Greenwood-Penny.

In 1922 another Army man, Captain Arthur Timms MC, took up residence at The Sycamores

Left: *General Percy Fortescue Gardiner (c.1890) retired to High Bickington after 40 years service in the Indian Army.*

Below: *Colonel Bernard Channer, c.1900, another ex-Indian-Army soldier who lived at The Sycamores after General Gardiner.*

with his mother and two sisters. They lived there until 1934 when they moved to a newly-built house called Broomhill.

It is not known if The Sycamores was until this time Church property, but in 1937 the Revd Gerald Jones became a curate in High Bickington and moved into the house. It then became The Rectory and remained so until the mid 1980s when the new Rectory was built on ground which had been tennis courts for The Sycamores. Today, The Sycamores has been renamed The Old Rectory and is privately owned. Today's Rectory no longer has a vicar in residence and the Diocese of Exeter has let it out.

For many years until Revd Wansbrough died the rectors lived at what is now Beechwood House. To quote from Kelly's Directory of 1889:

The Rectory [is] a substantial modern residence, with well wooded grounds [and] is situated on an eminence overlooking the Taw Valley, which affords an extensive view of the beautiful scenery of the neighbourhood.

The house stands above Nethergrove and although it can no longer be described as 'modern' it is very much a gentleman's residence with the aristocratic feel of wealth and the genteel way of life.

As with the Rectory, this house was some distance outside the village and I would have thought rather inaccessible to the parishioners. However, we must not forget that in those days, unlike today, the rector was considered one of the gentry, and however kindly he was the boundary between classes was evident - no more so than with this grand house away from the village.

It has been a popular theory that the house was built by the Revd Wansbrough's wife, as she was a

Letter from Mrs Gardiner to Revd Jones. After her husband died she moved to Bishops Teignton where she lived for another 50 years.

The lane outside Nethergrove, c.1930. On the left is Nethergrove Lodge and on the right is Rectory Lodge where Bill Davis, the gardener and chauffeur, lived. Mrs Davis and daughter Joan can be seen in the road. (R.L.K.)

Mr and Mrs Morrish, who lived at Nethergrove Lodge, c.1915.

lady of 'means' and did not want to live in the village. However, many previous rectors had in fact lived here and she no doubt had it rebuilt or extended.

We do know from local people's memories that she assumed the life of the lady of the manor. Rose Setherton (née Eastman) went to work for Mrs Wansbrough as a housemaid when she left school at the age of 14. Her sister Winnie was the cook and Louie Turner the parlourmaid. Rose remembers the day Bill Davis the chauffeur-cum-handyman collected her from home with her tin box containing all of her belongings. She lived in and got ten shillings a month (paid once every three months). On Sundays the girls had to attend church for the morning service even if it was their day off.

Mrs Wansbrough was a very strict employer (remember the story of the fire at Parsonage Farm, where the girls were not allowed admirers?). She also expected her word to be obeyed to the last letter and if tasks around the house were not done to her satisfaction she wasted no time informing the member of staff concerned. Rose recalled that there was a great deal of entertaining at the Rectory during these years, with dinners, garden parties and tennis parties, and Mrs Wansbrough expected perfection for her guests. However, she gave the staff an annual day out at her expense, as every year Bill Davis took the girls on a day trip to Exmouth.

When Rose married Walter Eastman in 1936 Mrs Wansbrough was unwell. Rose was told that after leaving her home in Atherington she must go to the Rectory to show herself to the rector's wife, before going to the church. This may have been the demand of a cantankerous old woman but I like to think it was the desire of a lady who had no children of her own and wanted to see a maid she was fond of in her wedding finery.

After her husband's death Edith Wansbrough remained at the house when The Sycamores became the Vicarage. In her later years she became mainly housebound. Doreen Ridd, who worked as cook and cleaner during this time, remembers the nurse, a Miss Alexander, who was a small elderly lady who insisted on having her afternoon nap. Sammy Couch was the handyman and Bill Davis was still the chauffeur. Doreen recalls that whenever Madam was well enough she would get Bill to take her to Barnstaple to see to any business that needed her attention.

It must not be forgotten that Mrs Wansbrough also donated the Church Hall to the village – which proves the point that the wealthy did take seriously their guardianship of those who were financially less well endowed.

No chapter on the gentry would be complete without mentioning Captain and Mrs Barton who lived at Little Silver, a substantial stone-built house with imposing views of the Taw Valley looking towards Portsmouth Arms. Jim Bright, who lives at Cross Park, remembers that his grandfather James Lee was a labourer who helped build Little Silver House in 1885. He lived seven miles away at Beaford and walked from there every day to start work at 7a.m. In 1889 the house was in the ownership of Edward Norrish Esq. of Sandford. The pedigree of Captain Francis Alexander Barton is not known but his wife was thought to be German and she studied music in Vienna. They were both interested in the arts and produced many plays and pantomimes for the village and school children. Nora Maynard remembers Mrs Barton well and told me, 'for an atheist she was a very nice lady'. She always put on a pantomime for the children at Christmas and afterwards gave them sweets and oranges.

The Bartons were the instigators and principal fund-raisers for the village hall, which was erected on North Road in 1920. The hall was named the Barton Hall after the Captain and his wife in recognition of all their efforts in procuring this establishment for the benefit of the parish. Did this spur on Mrs Wansbrough to provide a bigger and better hall for the centre of the village? Fund-raising had started in 1913 when the Bartons had held a Montenegrin Fête

Left: *Montenegrin Fête in the grounds of Kingford Hill House, the home at the time of Captain and Mrs Barton, 1913. Back row: far left is Gwendoline Hellyer and third from the left is Letitia Tucker.*

Little Silver House, soon after it was built, c.1898.

Women's Institute Garden Party at Old Park, c.1930.
Left to right, back row: ?, Mrs Davis, Mrs Cole, Mrs Pincombe, Mrs Harris, Mrs L. Pidler, Mrs Baker,
Mrs Hookway, Mrs Grossling; middle: Mrs Cook, Mrs Marcom, Mrs Good, Mrs Heales, Mrs Eastman,
Miss Kent, Mrs Gooding, Mrs Woollacott, Mrs Bull;
front: Doris Gooding, Mrs Laramy,
Georgina Wonnacott.

*This photo is entitled 'Captain and Mrs Barton's Staff at Little Silver Exhibition July 30th 1902'.
However, there are several people in it that were not staff. Left to right, back row: ?, Bill Slee,
Bill Newbery, Revd Wansbrough, Robert Gill Pidler, Bernard Cole; 3rd row: ?, Emma Tucker,
Elizabeth Cole, Mrs Newbery, Polly Tucker, ?, Sarah Cole; 2nd row: ?, Eva Pidler, Ethel Tucker,
Ada Pidler, Liz Goss, Lizzie Cole; front: Georgie Rawle, Letitia Tucker, Mary Tucker, Annie Tucker.*

*Little Silver Retirement Home bedecked with flags and balloons for the Millennium Over-60s Cream
Tea Garden Party, 2000. (A.S.)*

Another fund-raising concert produced by the Barton family. Third from the left: Letitia Tucker; fourth from the left: Miss Frances Barton; sixth from left: Miss Audrey Barton. Photograph, c.1918.

Children's Fancy Dress at the Rectory (Beechwood) Fête, 1918.

Above left: *Beechwood House which was the Rectory for many years, 1999.*

Above: *Old Park today showing the path Mrs Douglas-Hamilton had made leading her down to the river to watch Capt. Timms fishing.* (A.S.)

Left: *Seen here at Old Park Mrs Douglas-Hamilton in the bonnet with her brother on the left and Captain Timms on the right of the picture.*

at Kingford Hill, where they were living at the time. The question begs to be asked why they were living at Little Silver from 1893 until at least 1906, then in 1914 at Kingford Hill, then back at Little Silver in 1920? Was there any truth in the rumour that the Bartons lost a great deal of money on investments in South-African gold? We know from the diary kept by Bernard Cole that on 28 March 1914 Captain Barton and his son sailed for South Africa. The mystery deepens. However, for whatever reasons, the Bartons returned to Little Silver and continued their philanthropic ways with the local populace. Today Little Silver House is a residential home for the elderly, owned and run by Dick and Barbara Winship.

Kingford Hill was a wooden bungalow built in the woods overlooking the hamlet of Kingford and of course the beautiful views of the valley. After the First World War, when the Bartons returned to Little Silver, Mrs Sholto Douglas-Hamilton rented the property for a few years. She was a widow, her husband having been killed in the war. She was wealthy and had the welfare of the villagers, especially the women, close to her heart. She was a member of the British Red Cross and was involved in appointing Nurse Stear, the first district nurse in the area. She also formed the Women's Institute here in High Bickington in 1923. She held the first Garden Party at Kingford Hill in June 1924, which was opened by Lady Fortescue to raise funds for the High Bickington branch. Along with many sideshows there was music by the Barnstaple Town Band and dancing by the English Folk Dance Society of which Mrs Douglas-Hamilton was a prominent member.

Fame did not leave Kingford Hill with Mrs Douglas-Hamilton's departure in 1924, as the next inhabitant was Francis Ballantyne the son of the author Robert M. Ballantyne who wrote *Coral Island* and *Young Fir Traders*. Arthur Davis, known as 'Kelly', was chauffeur and gardener for the family. Kingford Hill today is a holiday complex.

While living at Kingford Hill, Mrs Douglas-Hamilton built Old Park, a large bungalow set on the hillside with views over the Taw Valley and Exmoor. It was here that many Women's Institute parties and schoolchildren's outings were held.

Mrs Douglas-Hamilton had a great interest in her garden, which she filled with seasonal shrubs. She died in a nursing home in Barnstaple only three weeks short of her 100th birthday, but her legacy of a beautiful house and garden and, of course, the Women's Institute, remains today. Lorna and Jim Ward now live at Old Park and they try to keep the house and garden in a manner which would have pleased Mrs Douglas-Hamilton.

The neighbour to Old Park is a red-brick house built in 1934 by the same lady for her friend Captain Timms. They were unable to marry as, under the terms of her husband's will, if she remarried she would forfeit his wealth. In the moral atmosphere of the 1920s and '30s it would not have been acceptable to live 'in sin'. Decorum was therefore maintained with the distance of a driveway from one house to the other. Captain Timms loved to fish in the Taw, and Mrs Douglas-Hamilton had a pathway cut from her garden down through the fields and woods so that she could ride down in her cart to watch him.

*Dr Augustus Greenwood-Penny with his father Robert at Nethergrove and
salmon they landed from the Taw, 1904.*

*Eli Harris of Weirmarsh Farm. He was a well-known horticulturist and churchwarden for 37 years
and also a keen sportsman and favourite on the hunting field. Photograph, c.1900.*

HUNTING, SHOOTING AND FISHING

Hunting, shooting and fishing were, in the 19th and 20th centuries, synonymous with the landed gentry. High Bickington's wealthy were no exception. The River Taw has always been known for its excellent salmon fishing and the hills on both sides popular with shooting parties. Robert Greenwood-Penny and his sons Robert Augustus and Sidney were respected field sportsmen – as were their cousins, Doctors Arnold and Thomas Saxty Good.

Mary Good wrote about Uncle 'Gus' and his brother Sidney coming to stay at Dobbs for the Spring fishing. They always caused confusion as they had little respect for time and it disrupted the household routine. Mary remembers her uncles as 'big' men with natural uncut moustaches, which were fine and silky. They wore plus-fours, they smoked pipes and had hearty laughs.

The larder would soon fill up with fresh salmon, which were cut into sections and sent off to friends and relatives from Portsmouth Arms Railway Station. Shooting parties were also catered for at Nethergrove where John Cole was employed as a gamekeeper in 1891. Today there are still shooting parties held during the season. These are mainly at Weirmarsh Farm.

Hunting is an emotive subject with those both for and against becoming very heated in their discussions. However, it cannot be ignored that hunting has played a large part in country life for many years in this area.

Torrington Farmers Hunt was formed in 1939 by a group of farmers and professional men who broke away from the Stevenstone Hunt in order to have more days hunting. The land covered is between the Taw and Torridge rivers and from the coast to Dolton Beacon in the east.

After running the hunt by committee for the first few years, Frank Heal was elected Master, a position he held until his death in 1977. Brothers Henry and Les Morrish, who live on the border of High Bickington and St Giles in the Wood, then held the joint mastership until April 2000. Ken Ford of Webbery helped them in their last two years. The current Master is Rory Knight-Bruce.

There are approximately 90 hounds and a few terriers, which are looked after by David Bevan at St Giles. The Master hunts the hounds three days a week in the season, which starts at the end of August when the corn harvest is over. Lawn meets are held on supporters' property and there are several held in and around High Bickington. During the Christmas holiday period there has traditionally been a meet at the Old George Inn.

In 20 years time when someone reads this book what will they make of this chapter in our lives? Will hunting still be a part of the countryside or will it have been consigned to the history books?

The hunt meeting outside The Golden Lion, North Road, c.1890. The chapel faces a different way today. Note the paraffin street lamps.

The doctor cousins at Dobbs after a weekend salmon fishing in the Taw, 1923. Left to right: Sidney Greenwood-Penny, Thomas Saxty Good, Arnold Saxty Good and Robert Augustus Greenwood-Penny.

Digging out the fox at Lee Barton, c.1910. Third from the left is Lewis Snell holding the dogs and Dick Tucker holding the fox. They had originally gone badger digging but caught two foxes.

*Picnic lunch during a shoot, 1902. Left to right: the gamekeeper, Sidney Greenwood-Penny,
Tom Good, Gus Greenwood-Penny, Mr Robert Greenwood-Penny and Arnold Good.*

Tom Miller competing in a gymkhana at Bales Ash, c.1940.

Right: *Eileen Thorne, churchwarden and keen horsewoman who lives at Parsonage Farm which was gutted by fire in 1929. Photograph, 2000.* (A.S.)

Left: *Graham Heal of Vaulterhill Stud preparing for a day's hunting, 2000.*

Below: *Isle of Wight beagle hounds at the beginning of a morning hunt at Sherwood, 2000.*

Above: *Les and Henry Morrish, 2000.*

Chapter 13
In Times of War

The parish remained untouched by air raids, blitz bombing and food shortages during the Second World War, and for those who escaped from the big towns and cities, this area of the English countryside was an idyllic one. There were, however, local men who went to both of the World Wars never to return and this chapter of the book stands as a tribute to all those who fell... as well as to those more fortunate individuals who returned.

FIRST WORLD WAR

In February of 1915 a six-day recruitment route march by the Devonshire Regiment took place in the rural districts. It started at Morchard Road and travelled through Winkleigh, where they had dinner, on to Ashreigny, Burrington and finally to High Bickington, where tea was provided. At Winkleigh the streets were decorated and the schoolchildren were lined up singing patriotic songs. However, the regiment had little luck so they moved on to Burrington where they managed to sign up one recruit. At High Bickington there was a meeting where a woman in the crowd shouted, 'Why don't they get up a regiment of women? I should like to have a go at the Germans'. There is no record of who she was, but the offer was declined!

In fact, only 13 men enlisted throughout the six days' march which continued on to Torrington, Langtree, Shebbear, Petrockstowe and Merton. Earl Fortescue later wrote to a newspaper thanking all those who had helped, but added that if persuasion failed compulsory conscription would be brought in.

There are now few people left in the village with memories of this period of history. Syd Squire, who was very young, remembers the soldiers billeted at Hope Cottage. He watched them put on their puttees – strips of cloth wound round leggings. The soldiers helped with harvesting hay for the horses in the war effort and Shires hauled the large oak trees, which were used for timber. Many of the woods around High Bickington were depleted during this time.

The ladies of the parish played an active part in the war effort as a notice in a newspaper in May 1919 shows. A Prisoners-of-War Fund had been set up and a committee arranged a monthly collection. Mrs Gooding was Treasurer and Mrs Wansbrough Secretary. Contributions were collected by Misses Ella Pidler, Primrose Leythorne, Carrie Cole, Mary Tucker and Letitia Tucker. Two Devon prisoners were adopted by the parish, Private Pike of Morchard Bishop and Private Dymond of Bovey Tracey. Parcels of food and goodies were sent to them fortnightly. The sum collected over six months was £26.5s.1d.

A group of men assembled in the grounds of The Sycamores, 1914. Was this the day of the recruitment march?

Left: *William Wonnacott, baker, seen here with his wife Lucy and children Tommy, Vera and Florence, 1914. William served with the Devonshire Regiment in France and Lucy kept the bakery and shop running as well caring for three small children.*

Right: *This picture was on the reverse of a postcard dated 17 December 1914. It reads: 'To all at Mill – with best love from Willie'. Left to right, standing: Bill Brownscombe, Walter (Gussie) Parker, Archie Quick; seated: Georgie James, ?.*

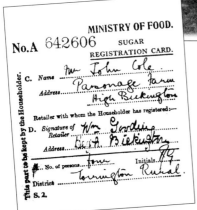

Above right: *George Squire of Loveham Farm, c.1914.*

Right: *Samuel Harris son of Eli Harris of Weirmarsh.*

Above: *Sugar ration card for the purchase of a limited amount of sugar each week from Goodings shop.*

Bottom right: *John Cole of Parsonage Farm (owner of the sugar ration card).*

SECOND WORLD WAR

There was more action in High Bickington during the Second World War. This time, we were warned, the enemy could arrive on our doorstep and Local Defence Volunteers - the forerunner of the Home Guard - were formed. Air Raid Precautions organised blackout material for curtains. Schoolchildren were taught how to put on gas masks and what to do in case of an air raid. As it happens there was very little enemy action here in the parish but the bombing in Exeter and Plymouth and along the Welsh coast could be seen by the fires that lit up the sky. With an airfield at Chivenor and one even closer at Winkleigh there was always the possibility of seeing action from the skies. Searchlights were put in place at the highest point of the parish at Sugworthy and on the most westerly point at Langridgeford.

There was excitement when one day in August 1940 a Spitfire crashed at Week Down, after shooting down a German plane over Beaford. The Spitfire pilot was brought back to a hero's welcome in the village and 'Ma' Gill gave him a bottle of whisky. Eric Bolt says there was quite a crowd gathered in the High Street and he remembers riding on the back of Jim Harris' motorbike to see the crashed Spitfire. Unfortunately, Jim was later killed in the blitz in London.

DOWN MEMORY LANE

When gathering information for this book we held a cream tea afternoon for people with reminiscences of the war years. For two hours the Church Hall buzzed with chatter and laughter. The following are some of the tales that surfaced.

The church had to have blackout material at the windows which was called 'sisal paper' and consisted of two pieces of brown paper with material in-between. Florrie Tapscott made the curtains and as you can imagine there was a great deal of material to handle. Reg White, Dick Tapscott and Syd Squire hung them up as roller blinds.

Schoolchildren wearing their gas masks had to enter a tent, erected in a classroom. Once inside they had to lift the side of the mask to sniff gas so that they would recognise what it smelled like - the First World War and gas warfare was still fresh in some people's minds. Keith Snell remembers that they also did gas-mask drill in a gulley in the far corner of the churchyard.

At the age of 14, Dick Pidler joined the Air Training Corps and managed to get himself a trip in an aircraft from Winkleigh Aerodrome. He reckons that because he was tall for his age and in uniform nobody asked any questions. Anyway he enjoyed the experience.

Italian and Polish prisoners of war were lodged at a camp in Chulmleigh and worked on nearby farms. Several kept in contact with local people after the war and some even chose never to return to their homeland.

On VE night there was much celebrating and 'Ma' Gill ran out of beer at the Golden Lion. The day was saved when Lewis Brownscombe produced from somewhere unknown a barrel of cider. After this had been consumed, Harry Webber decided that the Union Jack should be hoisted on the flagpole attached to the pub roof, so he climbed up unaided and did the honours.

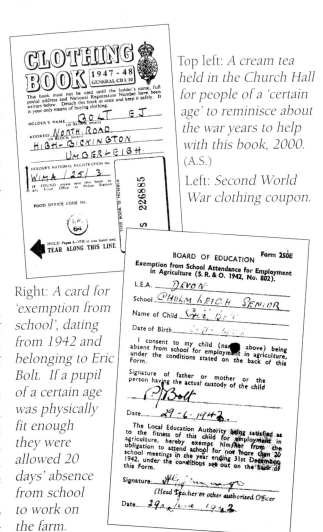

Top left: *A cream tea held in the Church Hall for people of a 'certain age' to reminisce about the war years to help with this book, 2000.* (A.S.)

Left: *Second World War clothing coupon.*

Right: *A card for 'exemption from school', dating from 1942 and belonging to Eric Bolt. If a pupil of a certain age was physically fit enough they were allowed 20 days' absence from school to work on the farm.*

Above: *Plaque in St Mary's Church.*

Above: *Sammy Couch, 1940, who after joining 'The Gloucesters' was transferred to the 'Black Watch'.*

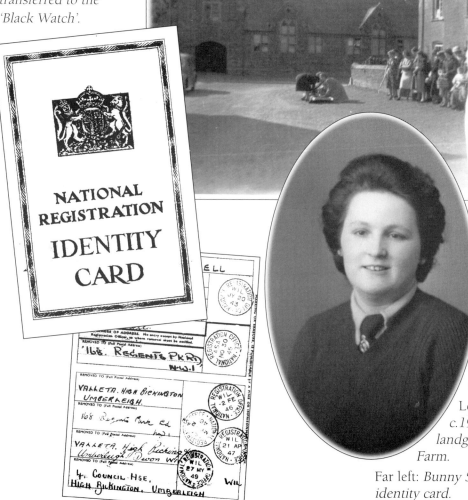

Top: *Ken Gill, 1940, of the Golden Lion, in his uniform.*

Above: *First-aid instruction being given by the Red Cross, c.1940.*

Left: *Mary Couch, c.1940, who was a landgirl at Deptford Farm.*

Far left: *Bunny Snell's wartime identity card.*

EVACUEES

On 4 September 1939 a large group of tired, bewildered but excited children from Sydenham in Kent arrived on the train at Portsmouth Arms Station. They were then ferried to the Church Hall. There were 88 children and four teachers, most of whom stayed for the duration of the war. Here are some memories of their visit to this village.

ALAN ASSHETON was only six years old when he arrived that September night. He and his brother Ken went to live with Stan Tucker's parents at North Road Farm. Alan remembers arriving in the dark and sitting on the floor of the Church Hall where there were lots of women bustling around. Mrs Tucker had said she wanted a sturdy lad to help on the farm now that her son had gone to war. However, she took two for the price of one as the brothers had to be together, no doubt because Alan was so young.

Alan Assheton during his war years which he remembers with so much pleasure, c.1920.

Alan vividly recalls waking on their first morning and looking out of the bedroom window at a grey horse, something he had not seen before. When he was told he could ride it he thought he was in heaven. He also remembers Archie Merrifield the blacksmith who worked across the road from the farm. Archie was a small, strong, friendly man and Alan loved to watch him work. After the war was over he returned to London, but the very next year when he was only 12 years old he went back to High Bickington - on a bicycle! He made this trip every year. It usually took him two days but on one occasion he did it in one! Later, when he married, he made the journey a permanent one and moved with his wife to Brayford where he still lives.

DON ASSHETON, Alan's eldest brother, was taking exams in the first year of the war and did not arrive in High Bickington until late 1940. He lived with Herbert and Doris Pidler at Dadlands and remembers them with great fondness. 'They were just like a Mum and Dad to me', he told me. He also recalls the great times he had on the farm with Sammy Couch who worked there. As Don was 14 years old he went to Chulmleigh School, which he did not like too much. One day he missed the school bus and so started back to Dadlands. When Herbert saw him he told him 'it just wouldn't do' and he would take him to school and present him to the headmaster. A very down-hearted Don was driven away from the farm.

However, Herbert passed Chulmleigh and carried on to Exeter where he gave him a guided tour of the city and a slap-up lunch. This included lamb 'fries'. When Don asked what they were, Herbert told him to eat up and he would tell him later. I can only guess that 'fries' alluded to lambs' masculine bits!

Peggy Field was 15 years old when war broke out so was not evacuated to High Bickington although her brothers ERNIE and DENNIS LATTIMER were. They stayed with May and Tom Miller at Great Deptford Farm and May remembers when the boys first arrived and all the men came in from harvesting for their tea. Dennis and Ernie were so shy they dived under the kitchen table. They loved their time on the farm. Peggy told me she came down from London to visit her brothers and wished she did not have to return. In fact, when she married in 1945, she stayed with May and Tom on her honeymoon, and returned on holiday with her children for 15 years running.

CHARLIE BALL was brought down to Devon in 1940 by his mother who was a 'clippie' on the London buses. She had made arrangements with Mrs Woollacott of Yelland Farm to look after Charlie. He told me that for the first three days he just sat and cried because he could not understand anything anyone said. His biggest enlightenment was when he found that milk came from elsewhere other than bottles! Charlie also told me of the time that he went shooting with Jim, using a Home Guard gun. They shot a rabbit but all they could find of it was its ears! He too says the Woollacotts were like family to him and he has kept in touch through the years. Like Alan Assheton, Charlie also eventually moved west. He now lives at the Lizard, Cornwall.

ROY HOPKINS and his brother DENNIS, who was five years his senior, travelled with the rest of their school on that September day in 1939. Like the others, Roy was also enthralled with living in the Devon countryside. However, the brothers were not so lucky in their first wartime home and had to be moved after a few months.

They were then billeted with Bill and Lily Parker and their children, Frankie and Jane, at Homewell, the cottage at the lower edge of the village. This move was to benefit the boys and remain with them for the rest of the lives. The cottage had no electricity, gas or mains water. Outside the front door, which was seldom shut and never locked, was a large flag-stoned

*A group of children evacuated to High Bickington during the Second World War, 1940.
Roy Hopkins is seated at the front cross-legged second from the left.*

*Alan Assheton with his mother helping with the harvest on one of his return visits to North Road
Farm, 1950. Joe Tucker is on the left and Stan is on the right.*

Dennis and Roy Hopkins in 1997 when they revisited the village 56 years after their evacuee days.

area in the middle of which stood a pump. Roy recalls that water had to be persuaded out of the pump by vigorous operation of the handle. They all washed under the pump and once a week had a good wash in front of the fire in a galvanised iron bath, filled with boiling water from pots and kettles on the range.

Roy and Dennis regularly had Sunday dinner with Bill's parents Ned and Polly; dinners which Roy describes as 'superb'. He says that unlike other parts of the country that suffered food shortages the same problem was never endured in High Bickington. The Parkers grew their own food and kept chickens for eggs and Sunday dinners. There was also a pig, which Roy watched growing over the year until he was a spectator at its demise.

He remembers their remaining time in the village with much pleasure, from Sunday School held in the Methodist Church (which Lil insisted they attend), to the evacuees' summer party in the Rectory gardens, and wandering down to the railway line at Portsmouth Arms with the other boys to watch the train going over pennies they had laid on the line.

Roy reflects that the time spent in our corner of the world was one of contrast. There was no wireless, television, telephone, running water, gas or electricity, and a bus only twice a week. But safety from villains and traffic, and the freedom to wander and discover were wonderful advantages. In fact a whole different way of life than he had known before opened up and left a lasting impression on him.

MARY HYMAS (née Graham-Pole) was the village doctor's second daughter and aged only two when war broke out. However, she has some vivid memories of these years. She remembers the Italian war prisoners being picked up outside Dobbs every evening and she and the other children would rush to the hedge to watch as they climbed into the back of a cattle truck. They had tanned skins and black hair and gleaming white smiles and they would wave to the children; but she would not wave back as she thought they were 'bad' men. With hindsight, she says, they were only young and probably had wives and young children of their own back home.

Mary, like most of the other children of that time, has fond memories of the sweet, silver-haired teacher, Miss Newbery, who they all thought must be at least 100 years old! Mary also remembers her gas mask in a little brown canvas case. She recalls the practices

they used to have at school and the warm, rubbery smell it gave off. Her family took in a little girl called Grace as their evacuee and she was completely lost and unable to settle until they located her sister and reunited them under the same roof. Mary cannot remember how long Grace and her sister stayed but it was long enough for them to lose their cockney accents and return to London with Devonshire ones.

THE HOME GUARD

Before the Home Guard was properly in place, there was a group of unarmed, disorganised, non-uniformed men who did their best to arrange themselves into a fighting force to be reckoned with. They were called the Local Defence Volunteers and were made up mostly of men too old to join the regular Army – hence the nickname 'Dad's Army'. However, what they lacked in youthfulness they made up for with enthusiasm and initiative.

Our men of High Bickington were just as ill-equipped as most other LDV groups throughout the country. There was no uniform, just an armband, and they even had to make these themselves. The only firearms were those they owned and, of course, the odd pitchfork came in handy. Later they were issued with a few First World War Lee Enfield rifles and taught how to load the ammunition by Army instructors.

As time went on the Home Guard became properly formed and the men were issued with khaki uniforms – although they left a lot to be desired in the fitting department. Here wives and girlfriends played their part in the war effort with needles and thread. The men were also issued with hand grenades, mills bombs, automatic rifles and sten guns. Gunnery practice was held every Sunday afternoon. There was a drill and exercise night during the week. The NCOs Reg Slee, Tom Blackmore and Syd Squire also had to attend at Chittlehampton for instruction. If the enemy had come the men of High Bickington's Home Guard may not have won the battle but would have made sure their adversary never forgot this ridgeway village!

THE 'TERRIERS'

A platoon of the Territorial Army was formed in High Bickington in early 1939. There were about 20 men from Atherington, Burrington and High Bickington and Sgt Major Walter Parker trained them in and around the village. At the outbreak of war the young men were enlisted into regiments of the British Army. Stan Tucker from North Road Farm joined the 6th Devon's at the age of 19. At the end of the war all of the men returned to their villages except Bill Down from Atherington, who was killed in Italy.

Territorials of Atherington, Burrington and High Bickington, 1939. Left to right, back: Roy Short, Edgar Cole, Bill Hanaford, Sgt Maj Walter Parker, Jimmy Parkhouse, Harold Brown, Gordon Short; middle: Arthur Jeffrey, Fred Harris, Stan Tucker, Percy Setherton, Ken Gill, Stanley Squire; front: Bill Goss, Herbert Kingdon, Bill Down, Sam Parker.

High Bickington's Home Guard, c.1940. Left to right, back row: J. Harris, J. Pidler, W. Clarke, C. Clatworthy, J. Woollacott, J. Tucker; 3rd row: L. Woollacott, E. Owen, W. Pidler, S. Farley, N. Rooks, J. Blackmore, E. Ellicott, W. Clatworthy; 2nd row: J. Turner, A. Short, A. Harris, B. Wythe, T. Courtney, D. Davey, B. Brownscombe, V. Parker, C. Shapland, F. Baker, D. Parsons; front: J. Headon, A. Tapscott, H. Gooding, H. and R. Pidler, R. Slee, S. Squire, J. Baker, T. Blackmore. (R.L.K.)

Chapter 14
Parish Pastimes

A century ago High Bickington parish was quite isolated and people therefore made their own enjoyment. The festivals of the religious calendar would all be celebrated, the best known, of course, being Harvest Festival. At Rogation time the parson and congregation toured the parish, and the fields, farms and people would be blessed. Another, lesser-known festival was the Plough Service. A plough was brought to the church to be blessed on the first Sunday in January. Until the 18th century the following day was a bank holiday. The plough was decorated and taken around the village and its health and prosperity were toasted by all and sundry. Drunkenness and other over-indulgences led to this celebratory occasion coming to a much-lamented end.

QUEEN VICTORIA'S JUBILEE

Other celebrations would be of the national kind; there were Armistice and Empire Days. In June 1900 to celebrate the taking of Pretoria during the Boer War there was a torchlit village procession with an effigy of Kruger fixed on a pair of wheels and escorted by guards. The route led to Little Silver House where Captain and Mrs Barton entertained the visitors with a firework display and refreshments.

Royal occasions also played an important part in village life. Queen Victoria's Golden Jubilee on 21 June 1887 was one such day. Police Constable Garland wrote an essay relating the day's events to General Gardiner's wife. He related that the day began at 9a.m. with a large body of men carrying a pole, 'with a representation of Reynard as its weather vane' to a spot opposite Mr John Down's residence where the pole was raised amid hearty cheering. The essay, which has been copied word for word and with as little punctuation as PC Garland himself liked to use, continues:

After the invigorating cup had been passed around the shooting party gave Reynard a parting salute, after which most of the people adjourned to prepare for the day's amusements, the decorations being pushed forward by a brigade of men under the directions of R.G. Penny Esq., the streets soon put on a gay appearance.

At 12 noon the greater portion of the parishioners had arrived and they were bent on having a jolly time.

At 12.30 noon service was held in the parish Church which was largely attended, the service was conducted by the Rev. E.R. Yerburgh Rector of the Parish, who preached an impressive sermon, his text being taken from the 25th Chapt. Of Liviticus, part of the 12th verse: For it is the Jubilee. The National Anthem was sung by the choir and the congregation, Mr. Ham presiding at the organ.

At 1.30p.m. the attractions became centred in a field belonging to Mr. George Tucker, where a large tent had been erected and beautifully decorated, and where a bountiful spread consisting of Roast Beef, Boiled Beef, plum pudding, cake, salad etc., was laid out by Bros' George and Nathaniel Tucker Inn Keepers who provided the eatables for the occasion, and who also provided a pint of beer, or a bottle of ginger beer for each adult, a cup of tea could also be had if preferred in stead of the above, the plum pudding was a gift of R.G. Penny Esq.

The following gentlemen presided at the dinner tables: R.G. Penny Esq., Major Gen. Gardiner, Rev. E.R. Yerburgh, Mr Eli Harris, Mr John Peake and Mr John Slee. At the rising of the first table, R.G. Penny Esq., gave a loyal toast of the day, which was heartily responded to, the Rev. E.R. Yerburgh kindly presented every male adult who indulged in the fragrant weed with an half ounce of tobacco before leaving the dinner table, after the adults had been catered for the children under 12 sat down to a substantial tea, altogether 505 were fed; after all had been served and all seemed satisfied with that part of the programme, and it being then about 4p.m., a move was made to a field at Little Bickington Farm kindly lent for the occasion by Anthony Garnish where the remainder of the day's amusements were carried out, it was at this time that business became entirely suspended, the shops and Public-houses were closed for the day, in fact everyone seemed to be moving in one direction, both old and young, rich and poor, all seemed bent in making the day a happy one, the village became almost deserted, it was like the

*Queen Victoria's Diamond Jubilee, 1897. This photograph was taken from the upstairs schoolroom
looking towards the High Street. The trees were planted in the road for the occasion.
The Revd Wansbrough can be seen in the foreground.*

A closer look at the jubilant crowd - only there are not many smiles to be seen!

1887

Her Most Gracious Majesty's 50 Years Reign.

The Jubilee Celebration on the 21st of June at High Bickington

A Free meal to all both great and small, With the following, motto

Come here and spend a social day
In harmless mirth and fun,
Let friendship reign be just and true
And evil speak of none

The Glorious 21st of June 1887, the day appointed for celebrating Her Most Gracious Majesty's 50 years reign, awoke as fine a morning, and was followed by as bright a day as ever Grace'd and English summer. The villagers of the ever loyal parish of High Bickington after a short night's rest's awoke with all the energy of new life and began to bestir themselves in making preparation for the celebration of the Glorious day. At 5.30. a.m. the first signal of the day's arrival being a volley from the fowling, pieces of a company of Farmers and Tradesmen, and at 6.30 a.m. the pretty peal of bells sent forth their melodious sound over the surrounding country, peals been rang at intervals during the first portion of the day, at 8.30 a.m. the village streets became full of life awaiting the next event, which was the raising of the memorial pole, with the representation of

one portion of the field a huge pile of wood and furse had been erected which was prepared for the bonfire, in another portion of the field there was laid out a race course staked and roped around, which gave one the impression that the Great Derby event was about to take place; it was there that nineteen splendid contested events took place in the running jumping tug of war etc. the most amusing races being the obstacle, potato & Tub, Three-legged, Driving the Wheel-barrow, blind-folded, and the Donkey race; the little ones were greatly amused by the fish-pond, where the delight of the little audience was great, when one of their number were fortunate enough to have a bite, and bring their fish to land in the shape of a box filled with goodies. At 6.30p.m. a greasy pole having been erected within the enclosure, with a large joint of beef attached to the top, many longing eyes were cast aloft to the prize, but only one young man had the courage to try and reach it, and after making several attempts, had to give it up like the fox did the grapes, it being too high, the young man Mr. F. Snell afterwards received the prize for his courage. About £5 was distributed in the prizes for the sports.

The Athletic portion of the programme having given ample amusements up to 10p.m., a light was then put to the huge pile of wood and furse, which soon became a blazing bonfire, the reflection of which could be seen for miles around, some of the young people indulged in tripping the fantastic toe, while others amused themselves by playing at kiss in the ring and other games.

At 11.30p.m. the village and parishioners all of whom expressed themselves perfectly satisfied with their day's enjoyment began to leave for their respective homes.

The day's arrangements were carried out under the directions of an energetic committee comprised of the following gentlemen:

Rev. E.R. Yerburgh, Chairman
Major Gen. Gardiner, Sec. & Tresurer
R.J. Penny Esq.
Mr. R. Pidler
Mr. Eli Harris
Mr. John Peake
Mr. James Harris
Mr. A. Garnish
Mr. John Slee
Mr. Tom Down
Mr.Geo. Tucker
Mr. M. Cowman
Mr. Tom Slee
Mr. A. Squire
Mr. William German
Mr. S. Dunn

hasty retreat of a defeated army, before its victorious opponents, leaving behind but the sick and wounded.

On arriving at the field it was found that every thing was in readiness for the remainder of the day's proceedings, at the entrance gate a temperance booth had been erected which was supplied by Mr. John Beer, and gave great satisfaction, in

The committee having divided into sections, each section having its particular of the day's programme to carry out, did their duty in such an efficient manner that not a hitch occurred in the day's proceedings, great credit being due to them for the enjoyment afforded during the day. Great credit will always be due, to the liberal way in which all subscribed, according to their means towards that great and glorious occasion. The subscription amounted to £36.6s.3d.

R.G. Penny Esq. with his usual generosity provided many things for the occasion, that the funds in the hands of the committee, would not allow them to indulge in.

In conclusion I would state that everyone conducted themselves with perfect sobriety, perfect harmony reign'd throughout the day, many of the elderly inhabitants stating, that it had been the pleasantest and happiest day, ever spent in the parish of High Bickington in their remembrance. And I feel certain that this glorious day's proceeding, will make many a pleasant fireside story for the little ones in years to come, by their loving parents who were eye witnesses to that days rejoicing, they will be able to tell them of their beloved Queen's 50 years reign, and how that great event was celebrated, by the ever loyal people of High Bickington.

God Save the Queen
I remain
Yours faithfully
John Garland
Dated the 18th of November 1887

My thanks to Edgar Cole for allowing me to use this notebook. I feel that PC Garland would be rather pleased that 113 years after he had penned his memories of High Bickington's festivities they were being used in a history book for generations to come.

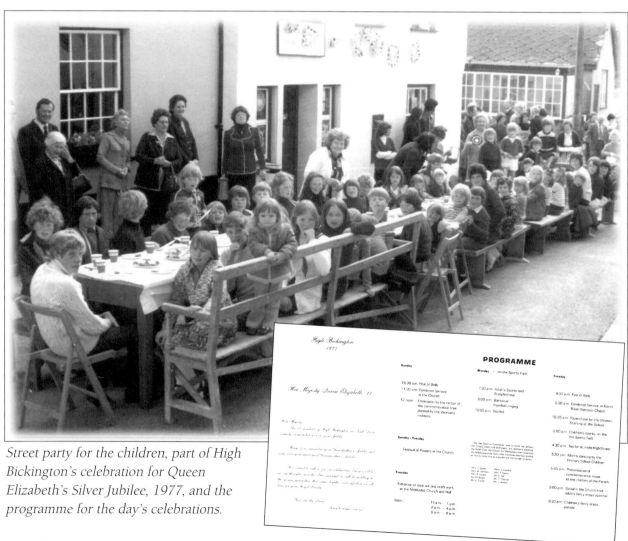

Street party for the children, part of High Bickington's celebration for Queen Elizabeth's Silver Jubilee, 1977, and the programme for the day's celebrations.

THE CATTLE FAIR

There were two ancient fairs in the village, the first on 14 May and the other on 2 October. After 1773 these fairs were discontinued, until the May Fair was revived in 1810 and held on the first Monday after 14 May.

This annual event was a great occasion in the High Bickington calendar. As we saw from the school logbook, either the children did not turn up for school or the rector closed it for the day. Cattle, sheep and pigs would be brought to the Village Square where they would be auctioned. Local lads earned their pocket money by helping to drive the cattle to and from the fair. To aid them with this task they made 'Fair sticks' which were usually hazel sticks that were cut and peeled to look like barbers' poles.

Everyone in the parish and beyond participated in this event. The ladies would be dressed in their best and provide the food for the men and children,

and no doubt the Golden Lion kept busy all day.

In the afternoon sports were held in a field at Little Bickington Farm. There were swings and roundabouts and the 6th Devonshire Regiment provided the band. Ice creams cost 1d. along with most of the rides. After the Church Hall was built the ladies also provided tea to complete the day's festivities.

The exact date of the last fair is uncertain but it was still going strong in 1939 when an annual cattle fair was held at High Bickington and the auction disposed of 400 lambs, store cattle and pigs. Three fields were also offered for sale but not sold. In the afternoon there was skittling and darts and a friendly football match against North Tawton.

The Hamilton Cup was competed for by boys and in the evening a grand victory dance was held in the Church Hall to celebrate the winning of two silver cups by the football team. The Hamilton Cup was a silver trophy given by Mrs Douglas-Hamilton for a 220-yard sprint race for boys under the age of 18. When won by the same boy three years in succession it remained in his keeping, a proud honour enjoyed by Peter Mitchell. After the cattle fair finished the High Bickington Athletic Club continued with the sports, football and dances and in 1949 the first carnival was held.

Cattle fair held in The Square, c.1945. Out of the picture on the right was the auctioneer. In the crowd can be seen Eileen Tucker, Bill Davis, Fred Pidler, Jack Down and the little girl with pigtails is Judith Squire. (By kind permission of the Beaford Archive)

A fête at Nethergrove, 1901.

WI meeting at Old Park, the home of Mrs Douglas Hamilton, c.1925. Left to right, back row: Mrs Davis, Mrs Dunn, Miss Timms, Miss Audrey Barton, Mrs Pidler, Mrs Cole, Mrs Gooding, Mrs Sowden, Mrs Baker, Mrs Tancock, Mrs Headon, Mrs Short, Mrs Facey, Miss Francis Barton, Miss Down, Miss Kent, Mrs Rippon, Mrs Eastman; middle: Mrs Marcom, Mrs Bull, Mrs Snell, Miss E. Tucker, Mrs Heales, Miss Ivy Slee, Mrs Pincombe, Miss Harris, Mrs Douglas-Hamilton, Mrs Good, Mrs Harding, Miss Taylor, Nurse Stear, Mrs Kent; sitting on ground: Elsie Heales, Miss Murch, Miss Olive Slee, Miss Maude Dunn, Mrs Harris, Mrs Tucker, Miss Miriam Harris.

Above: *Boy Scout Camp at Buckland Filleigh, 1918/19. Left to right, back: Herbert Pidler, Mr Brown, ?;*
middle: Robert Ellicott, Beert Wythe, Clifford Gooding, ?; front: Sam Naylor, ?, Arthur Snell.

BOY SCOUTS

A Boy Scout troop was formed in 1921 and Lieutenant Brimacombe, late of the Royal Navy, was the scoutmaster. Their first sports event at Chittlehamholt was a roaring success for Herbert Pidler who either won or was placed in most events. There is no record of how long this troop lasted but in the Church Council book I see that another troop was formed in 1952 under the leadership of Police Constable Swift.

WOMEN'S INSTITUTE

High Bickington Women's Institute, formed in 1923, is one of the oldest in the region. It is believed that Mrs Douglas-Hamilton was the first President and Mrs Mollie Good the doctor's wife was Secretary. The Institute was a welcome opportunity for the country ladies to socialise locally, while being part of a nation-wide educational organisation solely for women.

Summer meetings were often held at the homes of the gentry, at Old Park, Broomhill, Little Silver, The Rectory and the Old Rectory, Beechwood. Other meetings were held in the newly-erected village hall. Music, drama, crafts and travel talks were popular

pre-war activities. The outbreak of the Second World War galvanised these worthy ladies into action. First-aid and bandaging classes were held. There were activities such as knitting, sewing for the Red Cross and St Johns, the collection of wastepaper, stamps and canned fruit and a savings group.

At Christmas and Easter presents were sent to all of the serving men from the parish and in January 1943 some £38.2s.6d. postal orders were sent to them. A stretcher was purchased for the local ARP and funds raised for a Spitfire and Bren gun. Lectures on food production and preservation – including jam making – were arranged, and the President Betty Good (Dr Good's youngest daughter) joined the Women's Land Army.

The Institute has continued to provide access to education in many forms, to acquire new skills, to learn and join in various sports and leisure activities and to debate topical issues of national importance before voting for or against WI resolutions. As part of the millennium celebrations the village's senior citizens were invited to a strawberry cream tea provided by the WI at Little Silver House.

Today, 77 years on, lively and well-supported evening meetings are open to all ladies and held on the first Wednesday of the month.

Left: *WI in the Church Hall, c.1975. Left to right, back row: two landgirls during the war, Betty Harpum, Marjorie Waldon, Ann Lawson, landgirl, Olive Pidler; 3rd row: E. Hulland, Greta Woollacott, Betty Clatworthy, Dawn Baker, Maud Blackmore, Nell Pickard, Jennifer Gooding, Eileen Tucker; 2nd row: May Miller, Joyce Underhill, Doris Tucker, Doris Pidler, Miss Hawkes, E. Lawson, Mrs Walker, E. Smith, Letitia Tucker, Bessie Newbery, Greta Squire, E. Dymond; front: Jennifer White, Mrs Snell, Christine England, Mrs Plummer, Gwen Gooding, E. Strachan, Freda Squire, Marion (Nurse) Stear, V. Boundy.*

Above: *WI meeting in the Church hall, 2000. (A.S.). Left to right, back: Jennifer D'Olley, Betty Harpum, Marion Halstead, Briony Sapstead, Stella Burrows, Eve Burke, Josie Maskell, Joan Toop, Betty Mitchell, Christine England, Jane Gibson, Eileen Lansley, Joyce Underhill, Greta Woollacott and Peggy Stinton; seated: President Jennifer Gooding, Treasurer Brenda Wood, Secretary Rosemary Munson, Minutes Secretary Jean Checksfield.*

Above: *High Bickington WI on their float at Torrington Carnival, 1978. Left to right, standing: Jean Smithson, Greta Squire, Christine England; sitting: Mrs Strachan, Marjorie Johnson, Freda Squire.*

Left: *Ladies of the WI with their canning machine, 1940s. Left to right, back: Ruth Mardon, Mrs Ellis, Mrs Owen, Miss Francis Barton, Mary Quick; front: Mrs Good, Ethel Tucker, Mrs Merrifield, Olive Slee, Mrs Gill, ?, Miss Timms, ?, Mrs Graham-Pole.*

HIGH BICKINGTON ATHLETIC CLUB

A public meeting was held in the schoolroom on 15 June 1937 to consider the formation of an athletic club. It was attended by members of the football club and sports club. The first officers elected were Chairman Lt Col Maxwell; Vice Chairman Revd Jones; Secretary Mr L. Woollacott; and Assistant Secretary Mr W. Gill. Committee members were Messers F. Heales, S.J. Tucker, A.K. Wythe, W. Davis, L. Brownscombe, R.W. Pitman, W. Parker and J. Kent. It was the first of many committees which have organised High Bickington Athletic Club down through the years to the present day.

High Bickington Sports Committee, 1909. Standing second from the left is Ern Quick and seated fourth and fifth from the left are Dr Good and Jack Kent.

Meetings were held once a month and the main purpose was to promote sport for the community, especially football, and raise money for Club facilities. Dances in the Church Hall were arranged every three months with bands like Vera Lee and Her Merrymakers. The entrance was 1s.6d. with refreshments at moderate charges. Miss Newbery supervised the refreshments.

By the end of 1937 the hockey club had joined and in 1938 the tennis club. It was not until 1948 that the cricket club joined the ranks of the HBAC, when Col Timms and Mr W. Couch were accepted on to the committee to represent the cricket team. They were given £25 to purchase equipment.

The 1937–38 annual report shows that the village had two football teams who had not had a great deal of success, though not for the lack of support and enthusiasm. The hockey team had only played three times and lost, and the tennis club was only just starting the season. It was regretted that the only sports events had been those on Fair Day, but it would be attempted to revive them again. However, the social entertainment had been so successful they would soon require a larger village hall. They had held eight events in the first 12 months of the HBAC.

Over the next few years the entertainment committee raised a great deal of money by way of dances and concerts for sports equipment, coach hire, insurance and, in 1946, toilets for the football field (which were then hired out to other organisations such as the Gymkhana committee). Also in 1946 Mr Newbery's offer to build a radiogram was accepted. A committee was formed to supervise its earning ability. Rental was fixed at 7s.6d. per hour for village functions and 10 shillings an hour for transporting it outside the village. It was free to members.

It was a particularly successful year for the football team in 1947. The whole parish was behind the team when on Easter Monday it went to Lynton for the final of the Holman Cup. North Road was lined with coaches to take supporters to the match and when they came home triumphant there was not a dry glass in the village.

In June 1947 the Club decided to hold sports, fancy dress, a tea and a social on the occasion of the opening of the bus shelter that Mrs Laura Woollacott had paid to be built (see Chapter 2).

This was only two years after the end of the Second World War and clothing coupons were still in force. The football teams were badly in need of jerseys and socks so the committee was asked to spare as many as they could to help out with the situation. (I would like to have been a fly on the wall when ardent football committee members went home to their wives to ask for clothing coupons for the football kit!).

In 1949 came the purchase of the sports field via a bank loan. The Jubilee Field was officially opened on 16 May by Miss Barton, who also kicked off the football match.

High Bickington's benefactress, Laura Woollacott, was in evidence again in 1949 when Revd Plummer read a letter to the Club committee in which she offered to pay for a pavilion for the new sports field. It was opened by her sister Mrs Symons, on 7 October 1950.

The sports field, now called the playing field, has had its ups and downs over the years. The pavilion stands a long way from habitation and so has not been spared the usual acts of vandalism prevalent in the 20th century. However, a great many men, women and children (a large modern playpark was added to the field a few years ago) still get pleasure from the use of this field. Football and cricket are still played here through their respective seasons and after a lull in the support of the football team High Bickington again won the North Devon Senior League Division One and were promoted to the Premier Division.

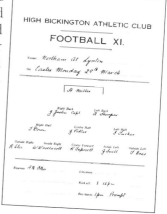

Early High Bickington Football Team in school playground, 1933. Left to right, standing: Dr Arnold Good, Clifford Gooding, Walter Parker, Peter Pitman, Wilfred Baker, Jack Laramy, Sam Naylor; seated: Bill Pidler, Reg Slee, Frank Dunn, Herbert Pidler, Wilfred Saunders.

High Bickington Cricket Team, 1950s. Left to right, back row: George Harris, Dougie Bale, Dick Tapscott, Pete Mitchell, Wilfred Mardon, Major Johnson, John Sowden; front: Joe Tucker, Bob Heale, Stan Tucker, John Snell, Reggie Johns.

Above: *Children on Sports Day in the High Street, 1946. Left to right: ?, ?, Mary Rocky, Julie Bright, Olive Parker, Sylvia Parker, Jennifer Gooding, Jane Parker, Phyllis Parker, Ian Slee, Linda Blackmore, ?, Stanley Parker and Gordon Merrifield.*

Inset: *The ladies who prepared the Sports Day tea, 1946. Left to right: Mrs Pickard, Mrs Shapland, Mrs Heales, school teachers Miss Tucker and Miss Newbery, Mrs Merrifield, Mrs V. Gooding, Mrs D. Pidler, Miss N. Cole, ?, Mrs G. Gooding, Mrs Good, Mrs Couch, Mrs Woollacott.*

Right: *The lads, 1946. Left to right: Ian Slee, George Owen, Gerald Squire, John Sowden, Keith Snell, Graham Gooding, Gordon Merrifield, Vernon Parker, David Huxtable, Alan Parker, Ron Saunders, Tony Turner. Note the Devon Constabulary sign on the Police House.*

*High Bickington team, the winners of the Holman Cup played at Lynton, 1947.
Left to right, back row: Charlie Woollacott, Albert Hooper, Jack Joslin, John Pidler,
Dick Tapscott, Tom Down; front: Reg Slee, John Snell, Herbert Miller, George Tucker, Tom Goss.
The man and woman on extreme left in the crowd are Jim and Florrie Mitchell and the man in the
centre with a bowler hat on is Jim Leythorne from Doric House.*

Above and left: *Eight buses line up in North Road to take the supporters to Lynton for the final of the Holman Cup and, on their victorious return, the trophy takes pride of place in Goodings shop window.*

Comic football match held during Fair Week, 1953. The men versus the ladies with the men dressed as women! Left to right, back row: Keith Snell, Reg Slee, Charlie Shapland, Gordon Merrifield, Charlie Brownscombe, Clifford England; middle: Jack Joslin, Peter Gordon, John Pidler, Peter Snell, Wilf Mardon; front: Joe Tucker and Sammy Couch.

The ladies' team dressed as men, 1953. Left to right, back row: Queenie Merrifield, Freda Patt, Jennifer Gooding, ? Blackmore, Lil Owen; middle: Christine England, Greta Squire, Florrie Woollacott, Diana Woollacott, Rosemary Jordon; front: Margaret Eastman and Janet Slee.

Below: Richard Tucker in action during a football match at the Sports Field, 1969. Victor Dadds is on his knee.

The High Bickington team, 1969. Left to right, back row: Gerald Herniman, Gordon Webber, Michael Parker, Les Morrish, Geoff Thomas, Clive Gooding; front: Keith Snell, Victor Dadds, Stan Parker, Richard Tucker, Roy Herniman.

Left: High Bickington cricket team, 1999. Left to right, back row: Chris Lintin, David Venner, Derek Herniman, James Lewis, Call Ozelton, Paul Richards, Josh May; front: Ian Rose with mascot Billy, Peter May, Andy Payne, James Lintin. (A.S.)

Right: *The High Bickington football team who finished the season on a winning streak, 2000. Left to right, back row: Tony Delahaye, Richard Maud, Nick Brown, Nick Squire, Edward Burns, Ben Beel, Michael Avery, Andrew Tucker; front: Jason Tapscott, Frank Stone, James Foden, Simon Green, Jason Kelly, Jonathon Tapscott, Ashley Underhill, Darren Avery. (A.S.)*

⁓ DONATIONS FROM LAURA WOOLLACOTT ⁓

Left and far left: *Opening of the bus shelter (1947) donated by Mrs Laura Woollacott (far left). Left to right, back: L. Woollacott, D. Millman, S. Davie, M. Gullett, L. Millman, M. Symons, Mr Lampard-Vachell, R. Pidler, J. Kent, J. Tucker, G. Kent, E. Adams, D. Davie, F. Woollacott; front: M. Gullett, J. Millman, M. Millman, P. Millman, D. Woollacott, S. Shapland, K. Davis.*

Above: *The opening of the sports pavilion, 1950. Back row lady in light coat is Eileen Tucker and lady on the far right is Mrs Douglas-Hamilton. Jack Kent is standing at the back. Left to right, front: May Miller, Doris Tucker, John Tucker, Jim and Greta Woollacott, ?, Mrs Laramy, Bill Laramy, Bill Pidler, Jack Laramy.*

Above: *Mrs Symons (Laura Woollacott's sister) at the opening of the sports pavilion on 7 October, 1950.*

Right: *Football match held on the day of the opening of the sports pavilion. Left to right, back row: H. Bosence, W. Baker, F. Parker, W. Avery, R. Mellows, J. Mellows; front: F. Keen, D. Lock, J. Pidler, J. Joslin, K. Snell.*

Stagehands and performers for High Bickington Concert Party, 1955. Left to right: Cliff England, Reg Slee, Bob Woollacott, Bill Pidler, Frank Parker, Tom Goss, Pete Mitchell, Bob Heale, Derek Squire, John Pidler, Sid Squire, Bill Norman, Walter Parker, Fred Huxtable, Sylvia Parker, Jim Mitchell, Dick Tapscott. The concert party toured the villages in the winter. The scenery was transported in Cliff Gooding's van and the scene shifters were Keith Snell and Dick Pidler. The leading parts were usually taken by John Tucker who always played the female and Florrie Wonnacott who always took the male lead.

Fancy-dress pageant held at Kingford Hill House, 1913.

CONCERTS AND CARNIVALS

As a quiet Devon village full of ordinary country people, tucked away from the artistic and theatrical world, an onlooker may be surprised at the number of concerts, musical recitals, plays and pantomimes the village has mounted. Admittedly in the early days it was the gentry who initiated these occasions and perhaps their influence followed down the years, as up until the 1970s High Bickington's Concert Party was well known and much sought after.

In November 1866 a Grand Amateur Concert of vocal music was held in the schoolroom. The room was adorned with scrolls inscribed with suitable Shakespearean lines. The Revd Septimus Palmer, his wife and daughters played a large part in the production and at the end of the proceedings they entertained friends at the Rectory. Mr Northway also took part in this production, and a newspaper review said his voice was 'too well known to attempt to describe it' - whether or not this was a compliment remains unknown!

From 1900 onwards for many years Captain and Mrs Barton took a leading part in High Bickington's theatrical career. There were plays, recitals and pantomimes for the children. From the 1930s, with the 'gentry' almost a thing of the past, concerts became the domain of the ordinary village people; and an excellent job they made of it.

In recent years Stella Searson, a concert pianist who lived at Beechwood House, often staged entertainments in the village. She and her husband Tony Rumbold also helped out with village concerts and pantomimes. They now live in France but returned in July 2000 to perform in a musical event 'A Romance of the Tudors' in St Mary's Church.

The first record of a village carnival I have found is in the Athletic Club minute book where it shows that it was agreed to hold a carnival on Fair Saturday, 21 May 1949. The first Carnival Queen was Marion Saunders in 1952. One of her attendants should have been Margaret Eastman but she contracted mumps and had to watch the procession from a car. The other attendants were Diana Woollacott and Sylvia Parker. In the early days the Queen was chosen by the number of 1d. tickets she sold. Marion Saunders sold 7000 tickets! Margaret Eastman had her day when she won the ticket-selling competition and became Carnival Queen for 1953 - the year that Elizabeth II was crowned.

During the middle years of the 20th century village carnivals were extremely well prepared and very popular. Local newspapers reported in full on the floats in the procession and people travelled from miles around to see it. For High Bickington it was the highlight of a week of activities, which culminated in a dance at the Church Hall.

The main organisers of High Bickington carnivals were Florrie and Bob Woollacott and unfortunately, when they could no longer carry on, the events were discontinued. The last carnival was in 1972, which means that Vera Herniman remains High Bickington's unchallenged Carnival Queen.

Silver Jubilee celebrations of High Bickington Athletic Club, 1952. Left to right, back row: Greta Squire, Gordon Merrifield, Lil Owen, Bunny Snell, John Pidler, Florrie Woollacott; front: Syd Squire, Sylvia Pidler, Reg Slee, Jennifer Gooding, Queenie Merrifield, Diana Woollacott, John Tucker, Christine England, Bill Norman. (K.P.)

Left: *Concert produced by Captain and Mrs Barton in 1920 in aid of funds to purchase a village hall.*

Below: *Bunny Snell applying stage makeup on Christine England in 1950 for one of the productions by High Bickington Athletic Club. Others in the picture are Queenie Merrifield on the left and Judith Squire on the right.* (R.L.K.)

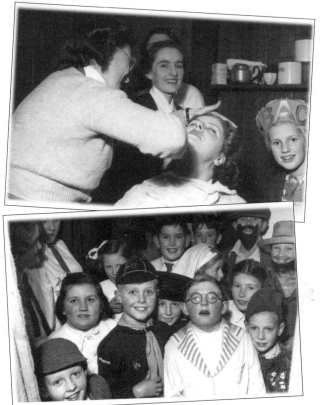

Above: *The first carnival held by High Bickington Athletic Club, 1947. A dance proceeded through the streets of the village to the tune of the Cornish Floral Dance and the occasion was completed with a fancy-dress competition. Left to right: Nora Cole, Joyce Stevens, Nurse Stear (with hat), Dot Gill, Ann Chapman, Sylvia Wythe and Sylvia Parker.*

Above right: *Children waiting in the wings before their entrance on stage, 1950.* (R.L.K.)

Right: *Another HBAC concert with John Pidler and Bunny Snell singing 'We can't stay here and get wet so try, try, try again', c.1950.* (R.L.K.)

Clockwise from top left: *Marion Sanders (1952); Vera Herniman (1972); Marilyn Woollacott (1970); Marion Goss (1965); Margaret Eastman (1953); Barbara Gill (1958); Vicky Smith (1968).*

Left: *Darby and Joan played by 'Ma' Gill and Tom Courtney.*

Below: *Barbara Gill as a lavender girl, 1951.* (R.L.K.)

Below right: *Colin Miller as a Red Indian*

Centre right: *Derek Herniman as a budding wedding photographer.* (S.H.B.)

Right: *The Terrible Twins - On the left Dennis Compton (Graham Gooding) and Bill Edrick (Keith Snell), 1947.*

Below: *Rosemary Jordan as Wendy, Peter Jordan as Captain Hook and Bunny Snell as Peter Pan, 1953.* (R.L.K.)

Above: *Uncle Tom Cobley, 1966. Left to right in costume: Dick Tapscott, Vic Dadds, Alan Trigger, ?, Doreen Ridd and Maurice Ridd driving his dumper.* (S.H.B.)

Above: *'Old Faithful' - Alan Pidner and his dog Riley.*

Above: *Wilfred Mardon on Mayflower outside Higher Deptford. He always led the carnival through the streets of the village.*

Right: *Andy Capp and Florrie - once again Greta Squire and Christine England.* (S.H.B)

Top: *'Southern Belles'. Left to right: Joyce Underhill, Mary Elliott, Ian Elliott, Dorothy Elliott, May Miller, Heather Goss.* (R.L.K.)

Above: *'Be Prepared', 1950. David Sanders, Geoffrey Peake, Ian Slee, Albert Kingdon, Clive Gooding, David England, Ronald Sanders, Bill Laramy.* (R.L.K.)

Above: *Punch and Judy - on the left Christine England and on the right Greta Squire.* (R.L.K.)

Left: *The Fancy-Dress Parade, 1955. In the crowd along with Police Constable Lane are Greta Squire, Christine England, Judith Squire, Barbara Gill, Dave England, Dick Tapscott, Barry Tapscott, Michael, Jimmy and Richard Tucker, and John and Keith Tucker.* (R.L.K.)

Top left: *Charity newspaper collection, 1997. Left to right: Kathy Manning, Mike Stone, Margaret Bolt, Eric Bolt, Hazel and David Pearce with Fiona Manning in the background.* (R.L.)

Above: *Dick St John with the result of one of his many hobbies, a wooden dresser which he designed and made himself, 2000.*

Left: *Eric Stone with his second(!) love – 'tinkering with motors', 1999.* (Both A.S.)

Above: *Geoffrey Rowden of Highfield, 2000. He has measured the rainfall every day at 9a.m. for 20 years.* (A.S.)

Above: *Thursday night is Honiton lace-making night at Brownscombe's Cottage, 2000.* (both A.S.)

Right: *Syd Squire turning a piece of wood to perfection, 1999.*

Left: *The Old George's Skittle Team, 2000. Left to right, back row: David Venner, Peter Worrall, Eric Stone, Colin Miller; kneeling: Andrew Barratt, Andy Payne, Barry Checksfield, Nigel Chase.* (A.S.)

Right: *The Old Codgers Cricket Team, 1999. Once a year they take on the High Bickington cricket team. Left to right: Andy Fenge, ?, Joe Humbleby, Bob Kingdom, Barry Checksfield, Greg Cannon, Brian Baker, ?, Eric Stone, Myc Riggulsford.* (A.S.)

Left: *The Golden Lion Darts Team, 2000. Left to right: Colin Miller, Lionel Wattingham, Derek Herniman, Richard Rosendale; front: Steve Herniman, Richard Enfield.* (A.S.)

Right: *The Old George Inn Darts Team, 2000. Left to right: Nicolas Cusden, Steve Upfield, Peter Worrall, Greg Cannon, John Reeves; kneeling: Simon Curtis.* (A.S.)

Left: *Jim Woollacott, John Tucker and Jim and Lorna Ward enjoying the view from Little Silver garden after their millennium cream tea which was laid on by High Bickington WI. The afternoon's entertainment was provided by a group who played old melodies and there were also handbell ringers and Karen and Reg from Seckington who played the bagpipes.*

Below oval: *Millennium baby Megan Pearce with mum Hazel and High Bickington born grandfather Eric Bolt.* (both A.S.)

Right: *The author's family watching the eclipse of the sun - live and also on television!*

Millennium Street Party.

Left: *A Parish Council meeting held in the Church Hall, 2000. Left to right in front: Alan Clemens, Roger Keen, Stan Maskell, Bernard Burke, Peter Tucker, Tim Webb; at the table are Secretary Diana Lunn and Chairman Maurice Ridd.* (A.S.)

Below: *Photographic exhibition, ancient and modern. Keith Snell and Victor Harris discuss a photo held by Richard Lethbridge.* (A.S.)

Left: *The Gardening Club held in the Church Hall, 2000.* (A.S.)

Above: *The Judo Club which until recently was held in the Church Hall, 2000. Back row includes: Instructor Bob Otto, Andy Angell, Gary Kingdom, Michael Down, ? Angell, Guy Newton, Amber Rose, Lauren Reeves, Dave ?; left to right, front: Charlie Finn, Chris Newton, Katherine Reeves, Phoebe Pidner, Shona Hardy, Zac Dodd, Alexander Phillips, ?, Jason Jones.* (A.S.)

Mrs Gill of the Golden Lion pulling the wishbone with Clifford Gooding at a dinner in the Church Hall. (R.L.K.)

Carnival tea party in the Church Hall in 1953. Ladies serving tea: on the left is Doreen Ridd, on the right is Carrie Sanders. The lady sitting at the table in front of them is Mary Parsons with her sons, from Gratleigh. (R.L.K.)

Group of ladies that provided the carnival teas outside the Church Hall, c.1950.
Left to right: Florrie Woollacott, Emily Woollacott, Betty Clatworthy, Gwen Gooding, Mary Couch,
Doreen Ridd, Christine England, Greta Squire, Hilda Courtney, Queenie Shapland.

Old Tyme dancing classes in the Church Hall, c.1950.
The girl looking up to the camera is Julie Bright. (R.L.K.)

*Three good friends. Left to right: Jim Tucker who married Bernard Cole's daughter Annie and
farmed North Road Farm, Archie Hellyer of Little Bickington Farm,
and Ernest Pidler who married Beattie Way of Kingford.*

*Left to right: Sarah Ann Cole, Annie Cole, Bernard Cole and, sitting in front, Elizabeth Cole outside
their house, Howards.*

Chapter 15
Local Characters and Families

Being part of a village is like being part of a large family; you may not want the others to know what is happening in your life but they usually do! This close interest can be daunting, but it shows that others care about you. Is it better to live where no one even passes the time of day? Or where people speak to you if they know you or not? The latter is what High Bickington folk have always been known for – friendliness. Here are some of them:

BERNARD COLE

Farmer and butcher Bernard Cole kept a diary that paints a vivid picture of the village in the first part of the 20th century. It contains a wealth of information from the state of the weather to cures for illness and, most importantly, events that made up the day-to-day life of a countryman.

Bernard was married to Sarah Ann and with daughters Elizabeth and Annie they lived at Howards, the house on the corner of the High Street and North Road. At the turn of the century it was a shop which sold everything from fat bacon to coal and china. Bernard was licensed to slaughter his own stock in the outhouses at the rear of the property.

Daughter Elizabeth married Tom Hookway and they lived at Ebberly Barton with their son Bernard. Annie married James Tucker and they started North Road Farm. They had three children, Ruth, Stanley and Joe. Today, Stan's son Peter runs the farm.

Bernard Cole was only nine when he left school. With Stan's permission I list some of his grand-father's note-form diary entries. They are just as he wrote them:

JUNE 21ST 1902   Capt Barton and family returned from Germany to Little Silver. Average price of Beef from 1st May to Midsummer 13/- per score.

1902   Coronation events for King Edward VII 250 adults took lunches in school rooms carried out by committee. 180 sandwiches cut for 100 children 50 left. Children fed in playground. Coronation events amount collected £42.11s.3d.

AUG. 2ND 1902   Mrs and Annie went to Minehead

AUG. 19TH 1902   William Pyncombe ordered

Bernard Cole at Nethergrove, c.1920.

to pay 10/- per week towards his wife.

OCT. 2ND 1902   Police Constable came to High Bickington.

NOV. 6TH 1902   Sir John Amorys Stag Hounds brought the stag from Molland and killed it At Higher House Farm Atherington. Stag weighing 15 score

MARCH 25TH 1903   Telegraph Office opened at High Bickington

SEPT 10TH 1903   Roughest weather for many years blew down all the apples and the roof of my haystack.

OCT. 6TH 1903   Capt. Barton and family left Little Silver.

NOV 23RD 1903   Bought pony colt from Fred Hellyer 18 months old for £9.0.0.

MAY 24TH 1904   Hugh Fraser Esq came to Little Silver to live. Capt Barton, 20 Burgerwise, Dresden, Saxony.

JULY 13TH 1904   Mr and Mrs Wood from America stayed 2 nights in High Bickington. Dr. Black specialist - Torquay - Cures Tumers and Cansers

OCT. 9TH 1905   Cook Jennett came to Rectory

MARCH 25TH 1906   Bought my house for £100

JUNE 28TH 1906   Rained from 7am to 8pm

George Perkins Fish Merchant, Rabbit game & poultry salesman, Birmingham

MARCH 4TH 1911   High Bickington 8 Bells rung for the first time. Colonel Channer Gave a bottle Whiskey to wet them.

JULY 15TH 1912   National Ins came into Force.

JULY 22ND 1912   Post Office time altered Mail bags brought from Umberleigh.

AUG. 24TH 1912   Very big land water, all marshes covered, but very little corn cut and What was was carried off

DEC. 6TH 1912   Preston Keeper caught Albert Turner, Dadland, shooting Phesants & picked up two dead ones. So A.T. had to face Col. Channer but denied all knowledge of it.

FEB. 11TH 1913   Roby Ellicott left H.B. for Australia sailed on Feb. 14th 1913.

APRIL 2ND 1913   Studley Brownscombe got locked up one night at Torrington for being drunk.

SEPT. 1913   In first week of that month Police Constable Tuplin killed a pig at 2 o' clock in the morning being bad he said.

AUG. 5TH 1913   Commenced altering my house - completed slate roof put iron railings around the front - made one bedroom more and made one more room down stairs and completed the job March 28th 1914 The cost of doing it £126 Noah Bird & Ernest Pidler did the work & gave good satisfaction.

MARCH 28TH 1914   Capt and his son Bartons sailed for South Africa.

JAN. 1ST 1923   Edwin Ellicott opened his butchers shop, started with side Beef only.

SEPT. 22ND 1926   New wood shutters in front of dwelling Howards.

1926 Coal Miners struck for higher wage on May 1st staying out for over 6 months and they did not get higher wage.

DEC. 29TH 1926   New Suit Clothes from Cooke Tailor Price £6.0.0.

SEPT. 7TH 1928   B Cole went to Old Park to Mrs Douglas Hamilton to lunch, being her birthday.

OCT. 18TH 1928   Mr W.B. Slee Butcher opened his new shop in North Road.

OCT. 19TH 1928   Mrs broke her leg & Dr Good set it.

SEPT. 16TH 1931   Stanley Tucker and Edgar Cole started school at West Buckland.

1933   What the prices was in 1933 to begin with it was a beautiful summer, good hay harvest & a good crop. And good Corn harvest... the yield good us ever known. Also good crop of potatoes. Best Beef all the year 12/- per score for the very best Mutton Lamb 9 & 10 pence per lb Hogs about the same price. Pork 11/- per score for the best size Wool from 6d to 7d per lb. A record

summer for fine weather, good time in early spring. A good time all through and the Autum and right up to Xmas remarkable fine.

MARCH 27TH 1934   Tom Hookway drove his new car Standard for the first time. A few of Bernard's cures for all ills:- Vapex from the chemist 2/- bottle. A disinfectant for colds and clears the head right away. Allcocks Porous Plaster good for weekness and pain in the joints. Put the plaster on and Let it stop on for 2 or 3 weeks.

Best thing known for travelling to prevent a person being sick. Eat a raw apple.

For Tom Hookways Indigestion Biscarted Magnessia Powder dose half teaspoonful in A wine glass of cold water after meals.

Good Cough mixture 4 ozs Cod liver Oil, 1 oz Honey 1 oz Glycerine.

Bernard Cole died in 1935 at the age of 85, so his hints on how to look after one's own health should not be sniffed at.

STANLEY JAMES TUCKER

Stan was born in 1920 at Howards. His sister Ruth later married Wilfred Mardon and they continued to live at Howards until 1999.

Stan started his education at High Bickington School and, as we saw from his grandfather's diary, he went to West Buckland School in 1931. Here he broke a thigh badly whilst playing rugby and was in hospital for ten weeks with his leg in traction.

In 1937 the Tuckers moved to North Road Farm where they have remained ever since. In 1939 with the outbreak of war Stan joined the 6th Devon Regiment at the age of 19. He served in Ireland, Italy, Austria, France and Germany. He was demobbed in Vienna where he remembers how cold it was. Stan was an Army driver but says of himself that he 'wasn't a good one' and that he was lucky to

Stan Tucker feeding his sheep after a sudden fall of snow, 1999. (A.S.)

come through the war unscathed, unlike some of his pals.

The young servicemen of High Bickington were treated like heroes when they returned to the village. Stan says he learnt much by his experiences away from home but is a country boy at heart and was more than content to return to the farm.

The farm has grown over the years and even after just celebrating his 80th birthday Stan still works alongside his son Peter. He hopes that Peter's two sons will carry on the family tradition in farming.

Stan has represented the parish on the Rural District Council and been a member of the Parochial Church Council. He has seen the village change from a self-supporting community who looked after one another and made their own enjoyment to one that is more commuter based. Stan remembers that when he was a child if there was any trouble in the village Mr Ham the schoolmaster, the doctor, parson or the policeman would sort it out. The authority of those men commanded the respect of locals but Stan feels that unfortunately those days have gone forever.

MAURICE RIDD

Maurice was born in the village of Morchard Bishop in 1933. He served in the Durham Light Infantry between 1950-55 and saw action in the Korean War. He has many memories of his exploits during this period and the life-long friends he made. After the war he moved to High Bickington where he married Doreen and lived at Cross Park. He worked for the next 20 years with a builder at Torrington, then became self-employed and worked in and around this parish for the rest of his working life. He was also a Special Constable for 30 years.

Now retired he never has a dull moment, as he has been a member of the Parish Council for 15 years and Chairman for the past eight. He has been a district councillor for 12 years and is on the National Association of Parish Councils – not forgetting being an advisor for the Citizens Advice Bureau.

Although Maurice spends many hours on council business he is often seen in and around the village tending to jobs that need doing. Now that a lengthman no longer visits the village, Maurice keeps the roadside verges free from debris and weeds. He cleans and repairs the bus shelter and the public seats, and if any elderly person needs transport to hospital or the railway station Maurice is their man! He is also on the 24-hour call-out scheme for any elderly person who needs help. Needless to say that all these tasks are voluntary and help to explain, Doreen says, why you seldom find him at home!

Maurice is a committed supporter of the under-dog and will always fight for what he feels is a good cause. He well remembers his childhood when his father was a farm labourer and they lived in a tied cottage. His father died young and Maurice recalls his mother being told two weeks after the funeral that they would have to vacate their home. 'Thank goodness those days have gone, never to return,' he says.

Top: *Maurice Ridd (in the centre) serving in Korea, 1953.*
Above: *North Road being attended to by council lengthman. This service has since been discontinued and Maurice Ridd seen on the right does the job voluntarily.*
Photograph, 1999. (A.S.)

NORA MAYNARD

Mrs Maynard lives in Atherington but was born Nora Hellyer, the youngest daughter of Stephen Hellyer at Little Bickington Farm, on 17 October 1904. The house Nora has lived in since she was nine years old has a 'White Hart' pub sign over the front door and long before Nora came there it was a public house owned by the parson. However, for many years her mother ran an off-licence here, as well as a smallholding.

You may wonder why a person who has lived nearly all her life in another village should get a mention in this chapter, but Nora has always felt akin to High Bickington and its people and attends any village functions. Her kettle is always on the Rayburn and it is an insult to refuse a cup of tea, as Nora likes nothing better than a chat. Her wit and enquiring mind make her a delightful person to take tea with.

On my first visit Nora told me she had four sisters, and a brother who emigrated to Canada many years ago. Her father was a farmer and a widower with children (she calls them 'the first family') when he married Nora's mother.

A photograph of her father, Stephen Hellyer, has pride of place on the kitchen wall; and a very handsome man he was. Nora says she can quite understand why her mother fell for him even if he had been married before and came complete with a family.

Nora has many fond memories of her young days in High Bickington, especially of school, where she loved the shows and pantomimes Mrs Barton put on for the children. She also remembers going to The Sycamores when Colonel and Mrs Channer lived there. She sat at the large table in the kitchen while the cook made cakes and let her lick out the bowl. Other memories are of Goodings Store, of the Post Office opposite where the Snell family lived, and of the blacksmiths, Frank and Wilfred Dunn.

Nora was nine when her father died and her mother moved to The White Hart at Atherington. She attended school in the village and was obviously a bright child as she went on to Barnstaple Grammar School. She was a weekly boarder and lodged with a family in Bear Street.

On leaving the grammar school she helped her mother with the off-licence and smallholding. For a while she became a schoolteacher at Atherington and when listening to her you realise just how much she loved this job and how much satisfaction she gained from it. She reckons she could not have been too bad a teacher because she taught Bill Seage and he still invites her to his house for Sunday dinner!

Nora married Roy Maynard who worked for the doctors at Dobbs until he joined the Royal Air Force during the war. They had two sons and she has been widowed since 1980. She puts her longevity down to the fact that the Bible says 'Honour thy father and thy mother', and she always did both.

SYDNEY SQUIRE

As I have leaned heavily on Syd's memories for this book the reader should feel well acquainted with him by now. He is 87 years old and lives with his wife Greta at Cross Park, High Bickington, the house they moved into when it was first built in 1949. You have heard about his school days and 'Slasher' Ham, his memories of local tradesmen, his apprenticeship with Whites the wheelwrights at Atherington and his war years in the village.

Now in his years of retirement Syd spends many hours with his hobbies and interests such as gardening, researching family histories, visiting traction engine rallies and, above all, working with wood. He loves nothing better than to disappear into his shed with a nice piece of yew, apple or pear, and to hone, turn and polish it until he brings out its natural beauty. He still has a great affection for the old wooden carts and carriages of his early days at work. He has remade and refurbished carts found rotting away in farmyards and also made a replica wooden cart from new which he proudly demonstrated at a local show.

It is the memories of people like Syd, who have had the time and patience to share them with me, that have made this book possible. So many times people have said to me that they wished they had listened to an elderly relative when they had been reminiscing, because once they have gone so have the stories. Hopefully in this book we have captured a few of them for posterity.

Syd in action in his home-made Governess cart.

FAMILIES

Well-known names in the parish such as Woollacott, Pidler, Tucker, Slee, Squire and Snell have been mentioned often in this book. However, another family which has had little mention are the Parkers.

Elias and Eva (née Moore) lived in the house now called Lyndale in Back Lane and it was here that they brought up 15 children.

Mabel Way dressed for tennis, c.1900.

James Parker, a great-grandson of Elias, has researched the family history and found that the Parker family originated from Winkleigh, a village seven miles from High Bickington. In the 1881 census Elias was 16 years old and working as a farm servant at Monkokehampton.

The 15 children of Elias and Eva were: Walter, Gertrude, Florence, Ned, James, Augustus, Anne, Maude, George, Eva, Fred, William, Sam, Jack and Beatrice. James died in the First World War, Gus joined the Army, George emigrated to Australia and Maude went to America. Florence married Percival Sergeant and settled in Barnstaple and Anne married John Heale from Seckington. Eva married George Brookes and had a son, Cedric, and a daughter, Sylvia, who lives in Exeter. Fred married Florence and lived in Exeter and William married Mary. Sam may have remained a bachelor. Beatrice married Arthur Jewell and had a son, Jack, who lives at Riddlecombe near Chulmleigh and a daughter Linda who married Charlie Bone, a butcher from Braunton. There were another two sons Henry and Jim and a daughter Christine.

The rest of the Parker family stayed in High Bickington and lived within yards of each other in the vicinity of Back Lane. Walter married Ivy Moore from Atherington and lived in a cottage attached to Parsonage Farm. They had two sons, Vernon and Michael (always known as Alan). Walter was a military man as was Alan who went to Sandhurst and gained a commission before serving 18 years in the Army. Vernon left Devon and became a patents' agent.

Walter was born in 1902 and joined the Duke of Cornwall's Regiment and in 1918 went to Ireland for the Irish Rebellion, after which he was posted to India. He left the Army and returned to Devon in the 1930s. At the outbreak of the Second World War he trained the Territorial Army group in the village before joining the regular Army again. He was once again sent to India where he fought in the Burma Campaign. At the end of his career he returned to

Devon where he died at the age of 81 in 1983. Walter is remembered in the village as a big man who was full of life and extremely fit.

Gertrude Parker married George Heale and they lived in Rose Cottage (as described in Chapter 2). They had five children of whom two daughters, Dorothy and Doreen, remained in the village. Doreen married Maurice Ridd and they still live here today. Jack Parker married Annie Short and they lived in Steps Cottage. They had four sons: Jimmy, Eric, Reggie, John and a daughter, Susan, who still lives in the village today in Poplar Terrace, no more than 50 yards from where she was born.

Last, but by no means least, there was Ned who married Mary Eastman, always known as Polly. They had two daughters, Gwen and Elsie, and a son, Bill (see Chapter 13).

The most descriptive piece of information I have received about Ned and Polly came from Roy Hopkins, an evacuee who stayed with Bill Parker during the war. He wrote that Bill and Lily's garden abutted the Parker senior's garden and Roy and his brother Dennis often found themselves in either house or garden. Grannie (as he called Polly) was a short, plump woman with jet-black hair, which occasionally she would unwrap and rearrange back into a tight bun. Roy was amazed to find that her hair when loose came down to her ankles.

Another memorable facet of Polly's life was her kitchen range. To a small boy the fireplace was extremely large; so large that he could walk into it and stand up. Part of the fireplace was occupied by a metal range. The oven section had doors and above the hobs was a series of metal levers, pulleys and hooks. With great adroitness for such a small woman Grannie would manoeuvre the heavy iron cooking pots on their hooks in and out of the flames and onto the hobs. Occasionally she would pause to spit in order to be rid of some unpleasant product of smoking Woodbines. In an instant this would sizzle and vaporise as it landed on the hot metal. As Roy says, it was a good job the pots had lids on!

Roy remembers Granfer Ned as an amiable rogue who retired after working as a farm labourer. He did occasional hedging and ditching and the money he got from this plus any more he could extract from his wife or by selling her chickens' eggs (without her knowledge) disappeared with him into the Golden Lion, to be converted into rough cider. Probably when the cider had had its effect Ned enjoyed telling Roy and Dennis vulgar stories. These involved the eructation of wind (in both directions) which he could do to order. Ned also had a great version of the escapades of the Oozlum Bird! These 'nature' stories were usually brought to an abrupt close by Polly's shrill call of 'Neead' which brought about a swift retreat of the Lesser Spotted Parker bird!

∽ THE PARKERS ∽

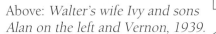

Above: *Walter's wife Ivy and sons Alan on the left and Vernon, 1939.*

Below: *RSM Major Walter Parker's discharge papers, issued 20 May 1945 in Calcutta. His civilian qualifications were water diviner and well sinker.*

Above: *RSM Walter Parker and his wife Ivy on the left, and George Brooks and his wife Eva (née Parker), 1945.*

Top centre: *Five of the youngest Parker children, c.1910 Left to right, back: Augustus and Fred; middle: Walter and Eva; front: Florence.*

Above: *George Heale and his wife Gertrude (née Parker), c.1915.*

Left: *L/Cpl Walter Parker during his first enlistment in India with the Duke of Cornwall's Light Infantry, c.1920.*

The Parker family at the wedding of Ned Parker and Mary (née Eastman), c.1910.

The Snell family before John, Lorna and Peter were born. Left to right, back row: Arty and Dion; middle: Kathleen, Betsy, Audrey, Gerald, Molly; front: Dorothy. Photograph, 1919.

Eli Harris later in his life seen here with his family at Weirmarsh. He died in 1926 at the age of 86.

Above: *Neil Tapscott in 1973, one of Dick and Jean Tapscott's six sons who lived in the house that had been The Commercial Hotel. Neil became a top hairdresser and had salons in Windsor and New York. Among his clients were royalty and famous sporting and show-business personalities. Singer Iris Williams once flew him to Moscow where she was in concert, to style her hair. Other clients included Shirley Bassey and Nick Faldo. Tragically Neil died in a car crash near his home in Windsor. This photograph shows him after he had won a competition at The Albert Hall.*

Below: *A Tapscott family reunion to celebrate Jean and Dick's Silver Wedding aniversary, 1974. Left to right, standing: Neil, Alan, Phillip, Barry; sitting: Mrs Florence Tapscott, Jean with Richard, Dick with Jonathan, and Denise.*

Left: *High Bickington's outstanding sport-woman between the 1950s and '70s. Jennifer Gooding is seen here in the 1970s preparing for a cricket match. She played for the Exeter Women's Team, Devon and the West of England Cricket teams. She began playing at the age of 20 and continued in competitive sport for 15 years. She also played hockey for the Westward Ho!, Exeter and Devon teams.*

Left: *Sammy Couch doing his weekly shopping, 1999.* (A.S.)

Below: *The Snell family at a wedding in High Bickington. Left to right: Audrey, John, Kathleen, Arty, Mrs Mary Ann Snell, Gerald, Molly, Peter, Dorothy, Lorna.* (S.H.B.)

Above: *Dr Ben Armstrong chatting to High Bickington's oldest inhabitant, Mrs Minnie Brind, 1999. Minnie, born in 1899, is still an active member of her community aged 101.* (A.S.)

Left: *David Venner, 1999, making a stone wall with a Devon hedge on top.* (A.S.)

Below: *Peter Tucker in 1979 with crew, aboard his quad bike doing the early-morning rounds.* (R.L.)

Left: *Bert Parsons as a child – he is sitting in front of his brother George and their father is standing on the right at Gratleigh Farm.*

Right: *Bert Parsons who was born and spent his early years at Gratleigh returns to High Bickington as a window cleaner.*

Above: *Marilyn Milton milk recording at Lower Farm, High Bickington.*

Left: *Designer and production engineer Ken Povey at work in his workshop at the bottom of his garden, 2000. His products are to be found in businesses at home and abroad.* (Both A.S.)

Above: *Plumber Andy Payne putting the lead flashing on the roof of a house in Barton Meadow Road, 1999.*

Left: *Shaun Clarke rethatching Brewery Cottage in Poplar Terrace, 1998.* (Both A.S.)

Left: *Myc and Jenny Riggulsford, 2000, who with the aid of the Internet, e-mail, fax and mobile phones can run their public relations consultancy just as easily from the heart of the countryside as from the heart of a city.* (A.S.)

Right: *Roy Brown who lives at Cross Park at work in the village on his JCB, 2000.* (A.S.)

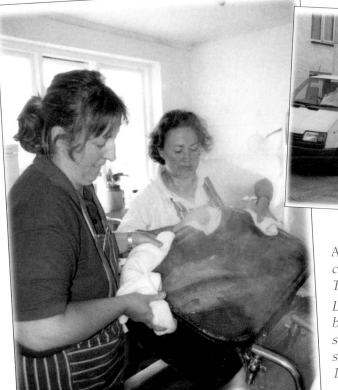

Above: *'A queue for Miles' mobile fish-and-chip van that visits the village every Tuesday evening, 1999.* (A.S.)

Left: *Sarah Payne, who owns a catering business, gets a helping hand from her sister, Sue Middleton, while poaching salmon for a wedding reception, 1999.*

Clockwise from top:
Maria Barratt, a trained hairdresser,
beautician and aromatherapist who is
a younger member of High Bickington
happy to run her mobile business from
her home at Doric House; painter and
decorator Gary Mitchell at work in the High
Street, 1999; Vera Stevens preparing lunch for
the children at High Bickington school, 1999;
the workforce of A.T. Motors, Jason, Jonathon and Alan
Tapscott. Alan competes in Rally X and has many trophies
to prove his success; Derek Herniman who grew up at
Libbaton Farm is now a bespoke furniture maker
and has his workshop far from
the 'madding crowd';
Visiting butcher
David Gratton
delivering to
Doreen Ridd,
2000. (All A.S.)

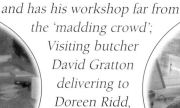

Left: *Photographer Rachel Phillips at work, 1999.*

Below: *Complimentary health therapist Roger Harris at work at Seckington.*

Below left: *Penny Povey who has a printing and anything-to-do-with-computers business. She is seen here welding a circuit board to assist her husband Ken in one of his engineering projects.*

(All A.S.)

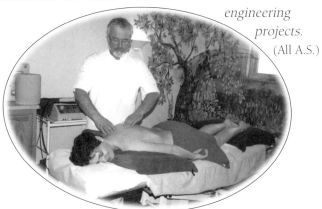

Above: *Thatcher's apprentice Rob Wilmot trimming the spar – a tedious but necessary task. Photo taken in 1998 when Brewery Cottage in Poplar Terrace was being re-thatched.*

Left: *Roger Keen our mobile greengrocer who grows much of his own stock, 1999. Roger is also a parish councillor and member of the Parochial Church Council. (Both A.S.)*

Conclusion

At the close of the 19th century High Bickington could boast three carpenters, two wheelwrights, a blacksmith, three stonemasons, two grocers, three butchers, three shoemakers (one also dealing with the post) and of course three public houses. At the beginning of the 21st century, it would appear that we are a lot worse off with only the Post Office, one print shop, two public houses and one village shop. However, once you have a more intimate knowledge of the workings of a typical Devon village and probably any village in this country, you realise that there is more than meets the eye on first sight.

I have found industrious folk at work, in sheds in the woods and in workshops at the bottom of the garden, in consulting rooms which were once, and outwardly still resemble, stables, and in transformed dining and sitting rooms – the most unlikely places being hives of sophisicated hi-tech office wizardary.

My conclusion is that life in the Devon village is not dead but very much alive and ticking in today's modern world. I do not suppose we will stun the world with any £multi-million deals, but we will enjoy living, and making that living, in this most desirable part of the world.

West Devon MP John Burnett joins High Bickington parishioners in front of the school to celebrate the new millennium, May 2000.

SUBSCRIBERS

Mrs Linda Aitken, Linlithgow, Scotland

Dr Ben Armstrong, Torrington, Devon

Don Assheton, Rustington, West Sussex

Crystal and Neil Atkins, Stowupland, Suffolk

Ellen M. Baker, Langley Barton, Umberleigh, Devon

Rachael D. Baker, Torquay, Devon

Raz and Jane Ball, Knossington, Oakham, Leicestershire

Harold C. Barnes, East Horsley, Surrey

Maria Barrett

John and Gillian Barthram, Barnstaple, Devon

Mrs E. B. Barthram, High Bickington, Devon

Natalie Barthram, Barnstaple, Devon

Tristan Barthram, Barnstaple, Devon

Richard and Margaret Beaumont, High Bickington, Devon

Sue E. Bickley, Umberleigh, Devon

Karen Blenkinsop, East Boldon, Tyne and Wear

Mr and Mrs G. Blewett, Kingford, Burrington, Devon

Graham Bolt, High Bickington, Devon

Heather Bolt, High Bickington, Devon

Eric and Margaret Bolt, Week Farm, High Bickington, Devon

Mr and Mrs D. Brown, High Bickington, Devon

Jane F. Bunclark, Shuteley, High Bickington, Devon

Hebe M.C.M. Bunclark, Shuteley, High Bickington, Devon

K. J. Burrow, Bucks Cross, Devon

The Burrows family, Welcombe, High Bickington, Devon

Alan and Petra Butcher, High Bickington, Devon

Linda and Greg Cannon, High Bickington, Devon

John and Ruth Carvosso

Gillian and Ken Cassidy, High Bickington, Devon

B. and J. Checksfield, High Bickington, Devon

Miss Louise R. Clarke, High Bickington, Devon

Denis J. Clarke, Pinhoe, Exeter, Devon

Alan and Noelle Clemens, High Bickington, Devon

Stella M. Corbett (née Boundy), Broadwood, High Bickington 1943-1960

Mr Sam Couch, High Bickington, Devon

Tony Cummings, High Bickington, Devon

Susan Dadds (née Farley), Barnstaple, Devon

Ines Dawes, High Bickington, Devon

Cliff and Jacque Dean, Witherhill Farmhouse, High Bickington, Devon

Mr Raymond Squire Debnam, Rayleigh, Essex

Mary Ann Delahaye, High Bickington, Devon

Robert and Judith Domleo, Fisherton Farm, Atherington, Devon

Kathleen Down, High Bickington, Devon

Harold G. Down, Barnstaple, Devon

Mary D. Down (née Wonnacott), Barnstaple, Devon

Rosa Eastman, Bishops Tawton, Devon

Father Patrick, USA

Mrs Betty Edworthy (née Good), Saskatchewan, Canada

Mrs Janet Farmer (née Slee), Crookham Village, Hampshire

Jackie Ferguson and John Dyer, High Bickington, Devon

Derek M. Fisher, West Down, Ilfracombe, Devon

Miriam Fitter, Dolton, Devon

Richard and Margaret Gayton, High Bickington Stores

Tom Gent

Adrian P. Gibbs, Paignton, Devon

Ronald C. N. Gibbs, Torquay, Devon

Peter N. H. Gibbs, Paignton, Devon

Mrs Jane M. Gibson, High Bickington, Devon

Carys Ann Gillett, Exeter, Devon

Revd Vincent and Mrs Carys Gillett, Exeter, Devon

David Gillett, Bath

David M. Ginns, North Heale Farm, High Bickington, Devon

Lesley Glover, Ebberly, St Giles, Devon

Mr and Mrs J. Glynn, Ramsgate, Kent

Miss Mary Good, Frome, Somerset

Jennifer Gooding, High Bickington, Devon

Dr John R. Graham-Pole,

Paul Green, Exeter, Devon

Dave Gumm, Ilfracombe, Devon

Mr and Mrs Ian Hale, High Bickington, Devon

Sylvia Hallett, Exeter, Devon
Marion and Brian Halstead, High Bickington, Devon
Pauline Hamblin
Betty Harpum, High Bickington, Devon
Victor J. Harris, Chittlehampton, Devon
Roger and Carolyn Harris, High Bickington, Devon
Gerald Herniman, High Bickington, Devon
Michael and Ann Heyes, Failand, North Somerset
High Bickington C.E. Primary School
High Bickington Surgery
John and Shirley Hill, High Bickington, Devon
Peter J. Hoare, Aylesbury, Bucks
Sandra Hocking, High Bickington, Devon
John and Wendy Hooper, High Bickington, Devon
Dr R. P. Hopkins, Oxfordshire
Sheila and Noel Humphries,
Mrs M. A. Hymas, Harrogate, Yorkshire
P. and P. Ingham, High Bickington, Devon
Mr and Mrs R. W. Jacob, Tawstock, Devon
Sue Jay, High Bickington, Devon
Mike Jay, Weston-super-Mare
Carole Jeffries, Bideford, Devon
Juliette and John Jenkins, East Preston, West Sussex
Betty Jensen Petersen, USA
Mrs Vera Jewell, Torrington, Devon
Steven Jones, Sittingbourne, Kent
Ada M. Kelland, Rose Acre, Yarnscombe, Devon
Paul and Tracey Knox, Rose Cottage, Kingford, Burrington, Devon
Rita Lambourne, High Bickington, Devon
A. Lawson, High Bickington, Devon
Richard Lethbridge, Chittlehamholt, Devon
Caroline and David Lintern, Sompting, West Sussex
Mr S. Lympany, Middle Barton, Chipping Norton, Oxford
Kevin P. Lynch, Barnstaple, Devon
Mrs Hilary C. Mackinnon (née Payne), Guildford, Surrey
Fiona and James Manning, High Bickington, Devon
Kathleen and David Manning, High Bickington, Devon
Martin and Carol Marks, Burrington, Devon
Pat Marsh (née Goss), formerly of Vauterhill & Meadow Croft Farms 1947
Josie Maskell, High Bickington, Devon
Mr R. McTaggart and Mrs T. Russell, Swallow Cottage, 1 Poplar Terrace,
Tom and May Miller, High Bickington, Devon

Mr and Mrs Colin Miller and Paul, High Bickington, Devon
John Milton, Georgeham, Devon
Mr and Mrs S. Milton, Moor Park, High Bickington, Devon
Yvonne and David Moorfoot, High Bickington, Devon
Rosemary Munson
J. Murch and Sons, Umberleigh, Devon
Betty A. E. Netherway (née Tapscott), Fremington, Devon
Philip J. Newcombe, Pilton, Barnstaple, Devon
Jackie and Toby Newth, Ebberly
The North Devon Athenaeum,
Judy O'Regan, Sandhurst, Berkshire
A. H. and H. J. Oakley, High Bickington, Devon
Mr Eric G. Parker, High Bickington, Devon
U. M. Parker, High Bickington, Devon
S. H. Parker, High Bickington, Devon
Katherine M. Parker, South Molton, Devon
Christine D. Parker, Barnstaple, Devon
Vernon Parker, Scotland
Joseph Frederick Parker, Barnstaple, Devon
James Walter Parker, Barnstaple, Devon
Sylvia D. Parkin, Barnstaple, Devon
Jennifer Parr (née Farley)
Marjorie M. Parrott, Henley-on-Thames
Bert Parsons
Hazel, David and Megan Pearce, High Bickington, Devon
Margaret Penton-Smith (née Joslin), Knowle Farm
Mrs D. M. Pidler, High Bickington, Devon
Pat Pidler, Barnstaple, Devon
Sylvia Pidler, High Bickington, Devon
Alan K. Pidner, Burrington, Devon
Robin Pierce, Wellington, Somerset
Robert Plummer, Barnack, PE9 3EA
Revd Hugh Pollock, Barnstaple, Devon
Mr F. E. Povey, High Bickington, Devon
Shaun and Kate Price, Country Ways, High Bickington, Devon
Tim Pugsley
Barry J. Raymont, High Bickington, Devon
John and Sarah Reeves
Adam Richards, (grandson of author)
Maurice and Doreen Ridd, High Bickington, Devon
Myc and Jenny Riggulsford, High Bickington, Devon
Ian Rose (Thatcher), Atherington, Devon
Jonathan Rowden, High Bickington, Devon
Linda and Geoffrey Rowden, High Bickington, Devon
Giles Rowden, Stafford

Maureen D. Rowe, High Bickington, Devon
Mrs Jackie Rudman, Georgeham, Devon
Mr R. C. Samyint, Libbaton, Devon
Carole Sanders, High Bickington, Devon
Marion Sanders (née Goss), Barnstaple, Devon
June Saunders, High Bickington, Devon
Kenny and Vicky Shaddick, Bickington, Devon
Rebecca Shaw, Wellington, Somerset
Ian R. Slee, Frampton Cotterell, Gloucestershire
The Smith family, Marlow, Bucks.
Martin T. Snell, High Bickington, Devon (1948)
Philip G. Snell, High Bickington, Devon (1943)
Andrew J. Snell, High Bickington, Devon (1950)
Gerald and Bun Snell, High Bickington, Devon
James and Sharon Spear (née Pincombe),
    High Bickington, Devon
Derek Albert Squire, Havant, Hampshire
    (family of Albert Squire)
Gary M. Squire, Portsmouth, Hampshire
    (family of Albert Squire)
Sydney L. Squire, High Bickington, Devon
Dick and Hannah St John
Lorna St John, Edgware, Middlesex
Gerry and Margaret Stevens, High Bickington,
    Devon
Mrs Vera Stevens, High Bickington, Devon
Ken Stinton, High Bickington, Devon
R. E. Stone, Colchester
Jack Stone, (grandson of author)
Ben Stone, (grandson of author)
Jamie and Tracey Stone, Barnstaple, Devon
Mr F. N. Stone, Ivybridge, Devon
Ian and Sharon Stone, Dishforth, N Yorkshire
Georgina Stone and Andy Martin, Barnstaple,
    Devon
Mr Desmond Symons, Fremington, Devon
Richard H. Tanton, High Bickington, Devon
Jonathan Tapscott, High Bickington, Devon
Allan Tapscott, High Bickington, Devon
Philip Tapscott, High Bickington, Devon
Barry Tapscott, High Bickington, Devon
Jean Tapscott, High Bickington, Devon
Richard Tapscott, High Bickington, Devon
Jenny Thomas, High Bickington, Devon
Philip Thomas, Sheffield
Claire Thomas, Barnstaple, Devon
Andrew Thomas, Devon
Eileen M. Thorne, High Bickington, Devon
Joan M. Toop, High Bickington, Devon
Keith S. Tucker, South Molton, Devon
John J. Tucker, Truro, Cornwall
Richard and Glenda Tucker, Lee Barton,
    High Bickington, Devon
Stan and Eileen Tucker, High Bickington, Devon
Ron Turner, Tiverton, Devon

Clive D. J. Turner, Millbrook, High Bickington,
    Devon
Joe Umpleby, Atherington, North Devon
S. J. Underhill, High Bickington, Devon
David Venner, High Bickington, Devon
John F. W. Walling, Newton Abbot, Devon
Mr and Mrs H. J. Ward, High Bickington, Devon
Sally and Tim Webb, High Bickington, Devon
June Webber, Burrington, Devon
Kathy and Roger Whitton, Cricklade, Wilts
Iris Wickett (née Ellicott), Barnstaple, Devon
Hazel J. Wickham (née Squire), Bishopston,
    Bristol
Mr and Mrs E. J. Winter, Port Mellon, Cornwall
Vida M. Wonnacott, Torrington, Devon
Alan Woodcock, Kingford, Devon
J. Woodhams, HighBickington, Devon
Mr A. J. Woollacott,
Jim and Greta Woollacott, High Bickington,
    Devon
Sharne Worrall, High Bickington, Devon
Margaret Wright (née Payne), Keyworth,
    Nottingham

*A quiet country lane that runs past Nethergrove,
from a postcard of 1933.* (R.L.K.)

ALSO AVAILABLE IN THE SERIES

SOME OF THE MANY TITLES
AVAILABLE IN 2001

For details of any of the above titles or if you are interested in writing your own community history, please contact: Community Histories Editor, Halsgrove House, Lower Moor Way, Tiverton Business Park, Tiverton, Devon EX16 6SS, England, e-mail:sales@halsgrove.com   If you are particularly interested in an image contained in this volume it may be possible to supply a copy. Please telephone 01884 243242 for details.